OUR

RADIANT

REDEEMER

TIM CHESTER

OUR RADIANT REDEEMER

LENT DEVOTIONS ON THE TRANSFIGURATION OF JESUS

Our Radiant Redeemer
© Tim Chester 2024

Published by:
The Good Book Company

thegoodbook.com | thegoodbook.co.uk
thegoodbook.com.au | thegoodbook.co.nz | thegoodbook.co.in

All emphases in Scripture quotations have been added by the author.

ISBN: 9781784989538 | JOB-007494 | Printed in India

Design by Drew McCall

CONTENTS

INTRODUCTION

Why read a book on the transfiguration? And why a Lent book on the transfiguration? Perhaps I can answer that by telling you why I wrote this one.

The transfiguration has always intrigued me. It's not really like anything else in the Gospels. There are plenty of miracle stories in which Jesus heals those who are sick or feeds those who are hungry. But the transfiguration doesn't quite fit that category—Jesus isn't helping anyone in need. The nearest parallels in the Gospels are probably the resurrection appearances of Jesus. But, while the risen Christ clearly has a transformed body, he looks like any other human being. He's not radiating light in the way he does at the transfiguration. The transfiguration stands unique.

And I'm attracted to passages I find weird! It could be that the Bible doesn't make sense, or it could be that there's a bigger significance waiting to be discovered. My policy is to assume the second option and dive deep into the weirdness! That's what I've done with the transfiguration, and I've not been disappointed. The transfiguration turns out to be a window onto so many important gospel truths. Here they shine—quite literally, for at the transfiguration, the face of Jesus "shone like the sun" (Matthew 17:2). On the mountain of transfiguration, the person and work of Jesus are on display in glorious technicolour.

This leads to a second reason why I wanted to look at the transfiguration. Paul says, "We all, who with unveiled faces contemplate the Lord's glory, are being transformed into his image with ever-increasing glory, which comes from the Lord, who is the Spirit" (2 Corinthians 3:18). We become more like Jesus—we're transformed into his image—by looking at his beauty. Looking at Jesus leads to being captivated by Jesus, and this in turn leads to becoming more like Jesus. We're changed by contemplating the glory of Jesus.

This is what drew me to the transfiguration. I want to be changed, and being changed means contemplating the glory of Jesus. So where to begin? The transfiguration looks like a great option. After all, this was the moment on earth when the glory of Jesus literally became visible as light radiated from his person. If you want to look at the glory of Christ, this is a great place to start.

But why a book on the transfiguration for Lent? After all, the transfiguration was done and dusted long before the beginning of the first Holy Week. The answer is that the transfiguration keeps pointing us to Good Friday and Easter Sunday. It provides its own distinctive camera angle from which to view the cross and resurrection. Perhaps that's not a surprise with the resurrection; we can readily imagine how the glory of transfiguration points to the victory of the risen Christ. But it turns out that the transfiguration also spotlights the message of Calvary. So the transfiguration is a great companion as we approach Easter.

This book is divided into weeks which correspond to the weeks of Lent. Each week focuses on one account of the transfiguration. Each day contains a devotion followed by a suggested meditation, usually in the form of a Bible verse, a quote or a hymn. The exception is Sunday (and the first Thursday of Lent). Each Sunday you're invited slowly and prayerfully to read the passage of Scripture that will form the basis of the rest of that week's reflections.

Don't worry if you get behind. You could use Sundays as a way of catching up. But in fact, it doesn't matter if you don't track with Lent and Easter. The transfiguration speaks to us every day of the year! It is a year-round invitation to be dazzled by our radiant Redeemer.

RADIANT

THE BEGINNING OF LENT

ASH WEDNESDAY

*His clothes became dazzling white, whiter
than anyone in the world could bleach them.*

MARK 9:3

Imagine a large plastic Santa in your town square.
It's been placed in some kind of tableau ready for
the run-up to Christmas. But, at the moment, it's
looking a bit lost in the darkness of the evening. If I
hadn't drawn your attention to it, you would probably
have missed it in the gloom. But then someone pulls
a switch, and an electric bulb turns on. From some-
where deep within itself, suddenly light radiates from
our plastic Santa, illuminating all around it.

By any estimation, the transfiguration of Jesus was an
extraordinary event. For a brief moment, it was as if a
switch was hit and suddenly light radiated from some-
where deep within Jesus, illuminating all around him.
"His clothes became dazzling white," says Mark 9:3.
Jesus was dazzling.

What was going on? Well, a lot more than we might at
first imagine—the transfiguration is a light that illumi-
nates the meaning of the cross and resurrection. As we
look deeper, we'll discover that it's not just Jesus who is

transfigured. His promise is that we, too, can be transfigured by the light he brings to our lives.

Ash Wednesday is traditionally a day on which to contemplate our sin. We look within and see not light but darkness.

We need light. We need illumination. We need Jesus.

The apostle John begins his Gospel, "The true light that gives light to everyone was coming into the world" (John 1:9). The light of Jesus is a metaphor: to "see the light" is to grasp an idea for the first time; we need light to ensure we follow the right path; or we say, "There's light at the end of the tunnel", to express a sense of hope. Light is a picture of understanding and hope. And light has come into the world, says John. Except John is talking about a person—the person of Jesus. Jesus himself is understanding and hope.

But on the mountain of transfiguration, that light became more than a metaphor. The light of Jesus quite literally shone in the darkness of our world.

Now come back to our plastic Santa. In one of the towns in which I used to live, the plastic Santa was well past his sell-by date! No doubt he had looked fantastic back in the day, but now he was shabby and worn. That wasn't a problem during the daytime, as long as you didn't look too closely. But at night, the light from within illuminated all the dirt and cracks. He looked worse with the light on.

With Jesus it was quite the opposite: the light revealed his glory and beauty.

It's our flaws that are illuminated and shown up by

the light of Jesus (John 3:19-21). I look ok, as long as you don't look too closely—as long as you don't hold me up to the light in the way you might hold laundry up to see if it's clean. But the light of Christ exposes my sin and failure. On Ash Wednesday, we come to him in confession. The light of the transfigured Jesus gives us understanding, and today that means an understanding of the depths of our sin. But, as we shall see, it also shines a light on the hope we have in Jesus. Even as we confess our sin, we can come before God with confidence because we come in hope, to find hope. "He is faithful and just and will forgive us our sins and purify us from all unrighteousness" (1 John 1:9). Here's an ancient prayer known as the Trisagion, which you can use to confess your sins:

Holy God,
holy and strong,
holy and immortal,
have mercy on us.

MEDITATION

This is the message we have heard
from him and declare to you:
God is light; in him there is no darkness at all.
If we claim to have fellowship with him
and yet walk in the darkness,
we lie and do not live out the truth.
But if we walk in the light, as he is in the light,
we have fellowship with one another,
and the blood of Jesus, his Son, purifies us from all sin.
If we claim to be without sin,
we deceive ourselves and the truth is not in us.
If we confess our sins,
he is faithful and just and will forgive us our sins
and purify us from all unrighteousness.

(1 John 1:5-9)

THURSDAY

The story of the transfiguration is told in Matthew 17, Mark 9 and Luke 9. We're going to start by reading Mark's version.

And he said to them, "Truly I tell you, some who are standing here will not taste death before they see that the kingdom of God has come with power."

After six days Jesus took Peter, James and John with him and led them up a high mountain, where they were all alone. There he was transfigured before them. His clothes became dazzling white, whiter than anyone in the world could bleach them. And there appeared before them Elijah and Moses, who were talking with Jesus.

Peter said to Jesus, "Rabbi, it is good for us to be here. Let us put up three shelters—one for you, one for Moses and one for Elijah." (He did not know what to say, they were so frightened.)

Then a cloud appeared and covered them, and a voice came from the cloud: "This is my Son, whom I love. Listen to him!"

Suddenly, when they looked around, they no longer saw anyone with them except Jesus. (Mark 9:1-8)

Take time to read it through a couple of times, preferably aloud. First time round, read it at your normal pace. Second time round, read it slowly, savouring each phrase.

- *What do you find striking?*

- *What do you find odd?*

Hold those thoughts. Hopefully we'll come back to most of them over the course of this book. In the meantime, here's a wonderful transfiguration prayer from a 14th-century monk known as Gregory the Sinaite. Make this your prayer as we begin to wonder at the story of the transfiguration.

MEDITATION

Today, in the light of your Transfiguration,
may we see you there as the Father's light, which never sets.
Enlighten our eyes
in the brilliant radiance of your divinity,
so that we may not fall asleep
in the darkness of eternal death.
Make the light of joy rise for us—
the light of truth and intimate knowledge.

O God, you light our darkened lamp,
our untended mind, the darkness of our ignorance,
to gaze on you and sing your praise and glory.
Let our minds be transfigured in the light of your glory.
Intoxicate us from the spring of your love,
from which, in the age to come,
your saints will be intoxicated
with the richness of your house.
May we be sheltered by the bright cloud of your wings.
May we be enlightened by the brightness of your energies,
but may we not be weighed down by that light,
due to our own unworthiness.
Lead us up into the mountain of vision;
shine on us like the sun;
appear before us through your goodness;
gather our mind and our voice towards you,
as you did Moses and Elijah,
and fill us with your glory.

(Gregory the Sinaite)[1]

FRIDAY

We were eye-witnesses of his majesty.

2 PETER 1:16

What exactly took place on the mountain when Jesus was transfigured?

In Matthew's account it's called a "vision" (Matthew 17:9, ESV). A vision can merely describe something that takes place *within* the mind. So was the transfiguration simply some kind of inner experience that a hypothetical onlooker would have missed?

Some sceptical scholars have suggested that the disciples created the story of the transfiguration to embody important truths about Jesus. The ideals of Jesus, they argue, transcend his time and what better way to express this than through a picture-story of Jesus being visibly transcendent. This approach is driven by the assumption that supernatural events can't happen within history. That prejudice then shapes how some scholars read the Gospel stories.

But it's clear that the apostle Peter did *not* see what happened on the mountain as a shared vision or an invented story. He knew the transfiguration to be a real event that took place within human history—and he was there! In his second letter, Peter explicitly rejects the suggestion that it was a "cleverly devised" story (2 Peter 1:16). Instead, he claims "we were eye-witnesses of his majesty" (v 16). "We ourselves heard this voice that came from heaven when we were with him on the sacred mountain" (v 18). Peter is like a news reporter on location. He's not relying on the accounts of other people. He's on the spot, telling us what he himself has seen and taking care to get his facts right.

However we make sense of what happened at the transfiguration, it *really happened*. Jesus really was transformed, and light really did radiate from him. It seems that Jesus deliberately went up the mountain with just three of his disciples to avoid being seen by too many people. (We'll explore why that was later.) But, in theory, if a shepherd had happened to wander by at the key moment, then he, too, would have seen Jesus transfigured; he, too, would have heard the voice from the cloud; and he, too, would have seen Moses and Elijah.

And while we're at it, what about Moses and Elijah? How did two dead men come to be standing on a mountain in 1st-century Palestine? As it happens, Elijah is one of just two people mentioned in the Bible who didn't die. (The other was Enoch in Genesis 5:24; Hebrews 11:5.) Instead, Elijah was taken up to heaven in a whirlwind (2 Kings 2:11-12). So it seems that Elijah was temporarily returning to earth. Moses did die. But there was some ambiguity about the location of his bodily remains (Deuteronomy 34:5-6), and Jude assumes his body was taken up to heaven by angels (Jude 1:9). The Reformer John Calvin suggests that God temporarily restored the bodies of Moses and Elijah with sufficient signs of their identity so they could readily be recognised[2], though we can't be sure exactly *how* this miracle was performed.

But it did happen. Peter, James and John were "eye-witnesses of his majesty". The majesty of Jesus is not a myth or a rumour. God himself, in the person of his Son, has stood on this earth—the same earth upon which you walk. Jesus is Immanuel: God with us (Matthew 1:23). The Father points to Jesus, as it were, and says, "This is my Son, whom I love. Listen to him!" (Mark 9:7).

MEDITATION

[The triune God] did not bid you soar
heavenward on your own
and gape to see what God is doing
in heaven with the angels.
No, this is his command:
"This is my beloved Son; listen to him.
There I descend to you on earth so that
you can see, hear, and touch me.
There and nowhere else
is the place for those to find and
encounter me who desire me
and would like to be delivered from sin and be saved."

We should quickly assent and say,
"God himself says this, and I will follow him
and give ear to no other word or message.
Nor do I want to know anything else about God.
For in his Person "dwells the whole fullness
of Deity bodily" (Colossians 2:9).
And there is no God apart from him
where I could come to him."

(The 16th-century Reformer Martin Luther)[3]

SATURDAY

*Two men, Moses and Elijah, appeared in
glorious splendour, talking with Jesus.*

LUKE 9:30

66 **Y**ou won't believe what's happening," says your
12-year-old: "Tom Cruise is coming to our
school". "Yeah, right," you reply. "I don't believe it; I
think you must have got the wrong end of the stick."
But then his older sister joins in: "No, it's true; the
headteacher announced it in assembly today". A
strange story from one person is easy to dismiss, but
two witnesses make you think twice.

We've seen that the transfiguration was an objective
event within history. This is reinforced by a striking
feature in Luke's account—one that's hidden by most
English translations.[4]

Luke's description of the transfiguration includes
the words "His clothing became white and gleam-
ing. And *behold, two men* were talking with Him"
(Luke 9:30, NASB).

Then, in his account of the resurrection, Luke describes
how the women came to the tomb where Jesus had been
buried, only to find the stone rolled away and the tomb

empty. Luke then adds, "While they were perplexed about this, *behold, two men* suddenly stood near them in dazzling clothing" (Luke 24:4 NASB 1995).

Finally, in his account of the ascension of Jesus in the Book of Acts, Luke describes how the disciples saw Jesus rise up into the cloud. Then he says, "And as they were gazing intently into the sky while he was going, then *behold, two men* in white clothing stood beside them" (Acts 1:10 NASB).

As Luke tells the stories of the transfiguration, resurrection and ascension, he includes the words "behold, two men" in each account, and each account also involves white or dazzling clothing. In the cases of the resurrection and ascension, these men are clearly angels, but Luke calls them "men" to heighten the link to the transfiguration. Each of those revelations of Christ's glory is accompanied by two witnesses. Two witnesses were the minimum legal requirement for evidence in a Jewish court of law (as set out in Deuteronomy 19:15). So the repetition of the phrase "behold, two men" not only links the transfiguration with the resurrection and ascension as revelations of Christ's glory; it also portrays all three events as legally verifiable facts.

When Jesus became human, he hid his divine glory in human flesh. Most of the time he looked like an ordinary man. He was, of course, an extraordinary man who did extraordinary things. But his physical appearance was indistinguishable from that of anyone else. "He had no beauty or majesty to attract us to him, nothing in his appearance that we should desire him," says Isaiah 53:2.

But for a brief moment at the transfiguration, the heavenly glory of Jesus was seen on earth.

In traditional icons of the transfiguration, Jesus is depicted on a rocky outcrop with a background made of geometric shapes: diamonds over squares over circles with lines radiating outwards. These shapes behind Jesus represent heavenly realities—we're seeing beyond the human Jesus to a divine reality behind him or within him.

Jesus is the gateway to God. The gap between heaven and earth is porous, and it's Jesus who is the portal between them. In the icons, the lines created by the rocks and the angle of the disciples all converge on Jesus. So our eyes are drawn to Jesus, but then, through Jesus, we see beyond earthly realities.

At one point Jesus said, "Very truly I tell you, you will see 'heaven open, and the angels of God ascending and descending on' the Son of Man" (John 1:51). It's an allusion to a vision the patriarch Jacob had in which he saw angels travelling up and down a stairway between heaven and earth (Genesis 28:12). Except that Jesus says *he himself is that stairway*. Earth and heaven meet in him. And for a moment on the mountain at the transfiguration, that truth became visible as heavenly glory streamed down to earth through Jesus.

Jacob's vision was accompanied by a promise from God: "I am with you and will watch over you wherever you go" (v 15). Remember that promise today. Let Jesus say to you, "I am with you and will watch over you wherever you go".

MEDITATION

*I bind to myself today
the strong power of the invocation of the Trinity:
I believe the Trinity in the Unity,
the Creator of the Universe ...
Christ with me, Christ before me,
Christ behind me, Christ within me,
Christ beneath me, Christ above me,
Christ at my right, Christ at my left ...
Christ in the heart of everyone who thinks of me,
Christ in the mouth of everyone who speaks to me,
Christ in every eye of everyone who sees me,
Christ in every ear of everyone who hears me.*

(From St Patrick's Breastplate)

THE RADIANT PERSON OF JESUS

THE FIRST WEEK OF LENT

SUNDAY

We've seen that the transfiguration was a real event. But what's its significance? What was going on as Jesus became dazzling white and the cloud descended?

We'll start answering these questions by exploring the precedents for the transfiguration. So ask yourself: where have you seen anything like the transfiguration before in the Bible story?

There are a number of possible answers. But the key precedent is found in Exodus 33 – 34.

> *Then Moses said, "Now show me your glory."*
>
> *And the LORD said, "I will cause all my goodness to pass in front of you, and I will proclaim my name, the LORD, in your presence. I will have mercy on whom I will have mercy, and I will have compassion on whom I will have compassion. But," he said, "you cannot see my face, for no one may see me and live."*

Then the LORD said, "There is a place near me where you may stand on a rock. When my glory passes by, I will put you in a cleft in the rock and cover you with my hand until I have passed by. Then I will remove my hand and you will see my back; but my face must not be seen."

The LORD said to Moses, "Chisel out two stone tablets like the first ones, and I will write on them the words that were on the first tablets, which you broke. Be ready in the morning, and then come up on Mount Sinai. Present yourself to me there on top of the mountain. No one is to come with you or be seen anywhere on the mountain; not even the flocks and herds may graze in front of the mountain."

So Moses chiselled out two stone tablets like the first ones and went up Mount Sinai early in the morning, as the LORD had commanded him; and he carried the two stone tablets in his hands. Then the LORD came down in the cloud and stood there with him and proclaimed his name, the LORD. And he passed in front of Moses, proclaiming, "The LORD, the LORD, the compassionate and gracious God, slow to anger, abounding in love and faithfulness, maintaining love to thousands, and forgiving wickedness, rebellion and sin. Yet he does not leave the guilty unpunished; he punishes the children and their children for the sin of the parents to the third and fourth generation" ...

When Moses came down from Mount Sinai with the two tablets of the covenant law in his hands, he was not aware that his face was radiant because he had spoken with the LORD. When Aaron and all the Israelites saw Moses, his face was radiant, and they were afraid to come near him.

(Exodus 33:18 – 34:7; 34:29-30)

Take time to read it through a couple of times, preferably aloud. First time round, read it at your normal pace. Second time round, read it slowly, savouring each phrase.

- *Can you identify similarities with the story of the transfiguration?*

- *Can you identify differences from the story of the transfiguration?*

Over the coming week we'll explore the significance of these parallels and differences.

MONDAY

The Son is the radiance of God's glory.

HEBREWS 1:3

In the TV series *The Secret Millionaire,* wealthy people go incognito into poor communities with a view to giving away money to what they deem to be worthy causes. Part of the programme's appeal is seeing whether anyone can piece together the signs and work out the millionaire's true identity.

The transfiguration is a big clue as to the true identity of Jesus. But we need to piece together the signs to work out what it reveals. One big bit of evidence is the link to the story of Moses encountering the glory of God on Mount Sinai in Exodus 33 – 34. Here are some of the similarities:

Exodus 33 – 34	Mark 9
"Show me your glory" (Exodus 33:18)	"Transfigured before them" (Mark 9:2)
Moses	Moses and Elijah (v 4)
On a mountain (34:4)	On a mountain (v 2)
A voice from a cloud (v 5)	A voice from a cloud (v 7)
"His face was radiant" (v 29)	"His face shone like the sun" (Matthew 17:2)
The Israelites are afraid (v 30)	The disciples are afraid (Mark 9:6)
"Tent" and "tabernacle" (35:11)	"Shelters" (v 5)

On a mountain in a cloud, Moses hears the voice of the Lord and (sort of) sees the back of his glory. And on a mountain in a cloud, the disciples hear the voice of the Lord and see his glory in Christ.

But there are also some important differences between the two stories:

Moses cannot see God's full glory (33:20-23)	The transfiguration is the full works
Moses reflects the radiance he has seen	Christ is the source of the radiance he emits
God speaks to reveal his own identity	God speaks to reveal Christ's identity

The transfiguration clearly mirrors the revelation of the Lord's glory at Mount Sinai, and Mark (along with the other Gospel writers) presents it in this way.

The transfiguration looked *forward*: it offered a glimpse of the glory Jesus would receive *after his resurrection*. But there was a lot more going on than this. The transfiguration also looked *back* to the glory of Jesus *before his incarnation*.

The echoes of Exodus 33 – 34 suggest the transfiguration is *all about seeing God*. The whole story of Israel at Mount Sinai in Exodus 19 – 40 is about Israel encountering God. Chapter 19 describes the safety measures the Israelites needed to put in place; otherwise "the Lord [would] break out against them" (v 22). There's no doubt that the people met the Lord, Yahweh, the living God.

Mount Sinai was an encounter with God. And if the transfiguration reflects Mount Sinai, then the transfiguration must be an encounter with Jesus as God. The glory of God is seen in the person of Christ. The disciples were given a glimpse of the eternal radiance of Jesus. His divine nature was made manifest in his human body. The disciples were privileged, says Don Carson in his commentary on Mark, "to glimpse something of his preincarnate glory and anticipate his coming exaltation."[5]

The theological term for a divine appearance is a "theophany". Moses experienced a theophany at the burning bush and on Mount Sinai. And now Moses experiences another theophany—in Jesus himself. God is made manifest in the human body of Jesus.

Mark says, "There he was transfigured before them. His clothes became dazzling white, whiter than anyone in the world could bleach them" (Mark 9:2-3). Matthew adds, "His face shone like the sun" (Matthew 17:2). This was inside-out rather than outside-in. When Moses encountered God at Mount Sinai, his face became radiant. The light of God's glory hit his face and radiated back to the people. Moses became, as it were, a mirror of God's glory.

But with Jesus, the light emanates from within him. He *himself* is its source. This is not someone else's glory; this is the divine glory of Jesus himself. The late Archbishop Michael Ramsey says that his "face shines not with a reflected glory but with the unborrowed glory as of the sun's own rays".[6] At the transfiguration, the spotlight is not shone on Jesus; Jesus himself *is* the spotlight.

Our first response must be to bow before Jesus, "the radiance of God's glory" (Hebrews 1:3). How will you worship him today?

MEDITATION

"[Jesus] briefly opened the door of his Incarnation for them, and showed them clearly what great glory was concealed within him."

(The 6th-century presbyter Leontius)[7]

TUESDAY

We have seen his glory.

JOHN 1:14

On 26 April 1986 the Chernobyl nuclear reactor went into meltdown, releasing a cloud of radioactive particles that spread across much of Europe. To contain further radiation, the reactor was encased in a massive steel and concrete structure. This has become known as the "sarcophagus", but its original name was the Russian word for "shelter".

When Peter sees the glory of God in Christ, he's scared—and his solution is a shelter.

Moses had been told, "You cannot see my face, for no one may see me and live" (Exodus 33:20). And now Peter is seeing the face of God in all his glory. Peter speaks, says New Testament scholar James Edwards, "as a hollow mortal in the searing light of the eternal".[8]

What's Peter's solution? To put Jesus in a tent! Peter said to Jesus, "Rabbi, it is good for us to be here. Let us put up three shelters—one for you, one for Moses and one for Elijah" (Mark 9:5-6).

The word for "shelter" is the same word for "tabernacle". Come back to Moses and Mount Sinai—how was the Lord of glory going to dwell among his people? By being contained in a tent. On the mountain Moses received instructions for the construction of the tabernacle (Exodus 25 – 31). The tabernacle meant that God was with his people. He lived in a tent just as they lived in tents. He had a temporary dwelling because he was on the move just as they were.

But at the same time, the tabernacle also *contained and constrained* the glory of the Lord. The danger posed by the glory of the Lord was shielded from the people behind the curtain of the Most Holy Place. The tabernacle made God safe. It made it possible for sinful people to live alongside the holy God. The tabernacle was like the concrete case that was placed over the Chernobyl nuclear power plant. The tabernacle protected people from the lethal holiness of the Lord. We need a tabernacle to contain God's glory and make it safe.

So Peter's instinct is *Let's put you in a tent.* It's a smart bit of biblical theology. But it misses the point: *Jesus himself* is the tabernacle. His own body is what contains and constrains the glory of the Lord. Jesus himself is the one who *safely* connects us to God.

"The Word became flesh and made his dwelling among us," says the preface to John's Gospel. "We have seen his glory, the glory of the one and only Son, who came from the Father, full of grace and truth" (John 1:14). The word "dwelling" is the Greek word for "tabernacle". "The Word became flesh and *tabernacled* among us," we might say. Jesus is not contained with a tabernacle for he *is* the tabernacle. He himself is the place where God and humanity meet—in his own person.

Jesus is the one in whom and through whom *you* can meet God *today* as you read his word and come to him in prayer.

MEDITATION

He deigns in flesh to appear,
Widest extremes to join;
To bring our vileness near,
And make us all divine:
And we the life of God shall know,
For God is manifest below.

(From "Let Earth and Heaven Combine"
by Charles Wesley)

WEDNESDAY

For God was pleased to have all
his fullness dwell in him.

COLOSSIANS 1:19

The transfiguration is a kind of visual aid to help us to see the divine-human person of Christ: divine glory radiating from a human body. In Christ, these two distinct natures—divine and human—combine in one person. This is the central tenet of an orthodox understanding of Christ: he is one person with two natures, or two natures united in one person.

This truth is taught in Scripture and was clarified in the early councils of the church, particularly the Council of Chalcedon in AD 451. The Chalcedonian Creed is affirmed by all the main branches of the Christian church so that "Chalcedonian christology" is another way of referring to an orthodox view of Christ.

The key statement from the Chalcedonian Creed is this: "We all with one accord teach men to acknowledge … one and the same Christ, Son, Lord, Only-begotten, recognized in two natures, without confusion, without change, without division, without separation."

"Without confusion, without change" means the incarnation did not create a third kind of being—some sort of God-man hybrid. Christ did not combine a bit of divinity with a bit of humanity to form a third kind of being. The eternal Son did not, for example, place a divine soul into a human body (as some people have claimed). The incarnation did not involve taking a human embryo, removing the soul and replacing it with a divine person. That would suggest a soul-less humanity (a body without a soul), which would not be fully human. Instead, the eternal Son took on human nature *as that human nature was formed in the womb* of Mary by the Holy Spirit. So Jesus is both fully divine and fully human.

"Without division, without separation" means the incarnation did not create two entities operating alongside one another—Christ is *one* person. The one divine person added a human nature to his divine nature without any reduction in his divinity and without any compromise to the humanity he embraced.

Think about the person who walked up the mountain with Peter, James and John. He had a human body just like yours. He grew tired as he walked. He sweated in the heat of the sun. Perhaps he asked the other three if they could pause for a moment while he caught his breath.

And yet the person who walked up that mountain had a divine nature that he shared with the Father and the Spirit. *He* is one person with two natures (a divine nature and a human nature); *they* are three Persons with one nature (a divine nature). "God was pleased to have all his fullness dwell in him," says Colossians 1:19. Even as he walked,

Christ was holding together the fabric of the mountain under his feet by his almighty word (Hebrews 1:3).

This means Jesus unites us to God not simply by dying in our place to overcome the problem of divine judgment against human sin—as central as that truth is to our gospel. Jesus also unites God and humanity literally *in his own person*. Where is the place where God and humanity are no longer separated but have come together as one? In the person of Jesus.

Jesus is the place where, or the means by which, we see God. We encounter God in Christ. Do you want to know what God is like? Look at Jesus.

MEDITATION

"Whenever one hears this Man's word
and sees his work,
there one surely hears and sees God's word
and work."

(The 16th-century Reformer Martin Luther)[9]

THURSDAY

"You cannot see my face, for no
one may see me and live."

EXODUS 33:20

The disciples encountered God in Christ every day they spent with Jesus, on every journey they undertook together, at every meal they ate together. But that encounter with God happened in a more *evident* way on the mountain of transfiguration. And it wasn't just a striking encounter for the disciples.

Both Moses and Elijah experienced major appearances of God, or "theophanies", during their lives. Both appearances took place at Mount Sinai or Mount Horeb as it was also known (Exodus 34:2; 1 Kings 19:8). Both involved God "passing by" before them (Exodus 33:19-22; 34:6; 1 Kings 19:11). And yet both experiences were limited. Moses said, "Now show me your glory" (Exodus 33:18). But God said, "You cannot see my face, for no one may see me and live" (v 20). So God placed both Moses and Elijah in a cave (Exodus 33:22; 1 Kings 19:9). He covered the face of Moses and allowed him to see only the "back" of his glory (v 22-23). He came to Elijah not in the power of a storm but in the whisper of his word (1 Kings 19:11-13).

This means that at the transfiguration, Moses and Elijah see God *for the first time.*

The request of Moses to see God is not answered on Mount Sinai. It cannot be. But it *is* answered on the mountain of transfiguration. Why? Because Jesus is there. God has taken on human flesh, and so now God appears before human eyes in the person of Christ. "No one has ever seen God," says John 1:18, "but the one and only Son, who is himself God and is in closest relationship with the Father, has made him known."

The 7th-century abbot Anastasius of Sinai imagines Moses responding to the transfiguration:

I see this great vision: you who have long lain divinely hidden from me, now revealed as God. You are no longer hiding your face, but I see you face to face and my soul is still preserved! I see you, whom I have longed to see from of old, as when I said, "May I see you and know you!" For your revelation is eternal life. I see you, no longer from behind, as I bowed myself down to Sinai's rock, but clearly appearing before me on the rock of Tabor. I no longer hide myself, as a human being, in the face of the rock, but I see you as the loving God, hiding yourself in my form ... For you are the mediator of old and new — God of old, yet newly human! You are the one who once revealed your name, invisibly, on Mount Sinai, and now are visibly revealed, transfigured on Mount Tabor.

The imagined speech continues with Anastasius (through the voice of Moses) attributing all the divine acts of the exodus story to the one who now appears before him. The Lord who rescued Israel from Egypt by sending the plagues and parting the sea is the Jesus who stands before Moses on the mountain. Moses ends by marvelling again that he has seen the God who cannot be seen.[10]

Perhaps you sometimes wish you could have been there when Abraham welcomed three strangers and found himself hosting the Lord, or when Moses stood before the burning bush, or when Elijah called down fire from heaven, or when Isaiah saw a vision of God in his temple. But we have something better, richer, fuller, bigger: we have Jesus. God has clothed himself in human flesh to reveal his glory to fragile, faithless human beings—like me and you. Thank him for his presence in you and with you day by day.

MEDITATION

The transfiguration was "a visible image of his deity" through which God "momentarily" revealed "the deity of His Son as in a living mirror".

(The 16th-century Reformer John Calvin)[11]

FRIDAY

"This is my Son, whom I love. Listen to him!"

MARK 9:7

One of the legends of mid-20th-century British comedy was Arthur Askey. One of his catchphrases was "Before your very eyes". It became the title of his first TV show and later his autobiography. I'm too young to have seen Askey "before my very eyes"! But his catchphrase entered my vocabulary through my grandmother.

At the transfiguration, the disciples see the glory of God *before their very eyes*. Mark specifically says Jesus "was transfigured *before them*" (Mark 9:2). The phrase "before them" suggests that this event was for the benefit of the disciples. Elijah and Moses are also said to have "appeared *before them*" (v 4).

There's another indication that the transfiguration is for the disciples. The words of the Father at the transfiguration are similar to his words at the baptism of Jesus, but with two significant changes:

> *"You are my Son, whom I love; with you I am well pleased." (1:11)*

"This is my Son, whom I love. Listen to him!" (9:7)

We will return later to one of those changes—the words "With you I am well pleased" instead of "Listen to him!" For now, let's focus on the other change; the words at the baptism are addressed to Jesus for his benefit ("You are..."), while the words at the transfiguration are addressed to the disciples for their benefit ("This is...").

The transfiguration did not provide new information for Jesus. Instead, it revealed his divine glory to the three disciples. The biblical scholar Joel Green says the point is "not that Jesus experienced an internal adjustment of some sort that led to his transformed appearance, but that his inner being was made transparent to those who accompanied him."[12] Or, as Michael Ramsey writes, "On the mount of Transfiguration a veil is withdrawn, and the glory which the disciples are allowed to see is not only the glory of a future event, but the glory of Him who is the Son of God."[13]

Jesus is on his way to the cross. The disciples will see him suffer horribly. It will seem as if his life has ended in failure. But the memory of the transfiguration will fortify their faith. Jesus "was transfigured *before them*" to reveal who he is when appearances will suggest that he is nobody. In that moment, they will fail to understand why Jesus is suffering. But also in that moment, they can look back to the transfiguration and hold on to that vision of his glory.

The same is true for us when we suffer. In the moment, we may not understand why we're suffering.

But in those times, we can look back to the transfiguration, and look up to Christ's ascended glory, and look forward to his glorious return. If this is you today, hold on to this vision of the glory of Christ and let his glory fortify your faith.

MEDITATION

Before thy Crucifixion, O Christ,
the Mount became like unto the heavens,
and a cloud was outspread like a canopy,
while thou wast transfigured,
and while the Father bore witness unto thee,
there was Peter, together with James and John,
inasmuch as they desired to be with thee
at the time of thy betrayal also;
that, having beheld thy marvels,
they might not be affrighted at thy sufferings.
Make us also worthy to adore the same in peace,
for the sake of thy great mercy.

(Orthodox Vespers for the Feast
of the Transfiguration)[14]

SATURDAY

Then a cloud appeared and covered them.

MARK 9:7

How do you feel about your body? The number of people on diets suggests that many of us wish our bodies looked different. Some people turn to cosmetic surgery to change their bodies. Our culture seems to have become ill at ease with the human body.

At the transfiguration, it is not just the glory of Christ's divinity that it is revealed; it is also the glory of his humanity.

Mark's account begins "After six days". Mark is sparing in his time references. He's a great fan of saying, *And this happened... And then this happened... And then this...* But he rarely specifies a specific time. (Mark 14:1 is the only other example.) That he does so here suggests he wants us to recognise that the sixth day is significant.

What else takes place on the sixth day? One answer is that humanity was created on the sixth day (Genesis 1:26-31). And now, in a way, God is doing it again. Just as Adam was the beginning of the old humanity—the humanity that fell into sin and became subject to death—

so Jesus is the beginning of a new humanity—a humanity free from sin and death. At the transfiguration Jesus is revealed as the new Adam. He is the one who is human as we were always meant to be human. And Jesus is the one who will restore our brokenness. The new humanity stands before us on the mountain of transfiguration and shows us what our new humanity will be like.

Mark says, "A cloud appeared and covered them" (Mark 9:7). The word "covered" means "overshadowed". It's the word used to describe the glory of God settling on the newly built tabernacle in the Old Testament (Exodus 40:35, Septuagint). The glory of God descended to fill the building. The same word is used in the angel's declaration to Mary: "The Holy Spirit will come on you, and the power of the Most High will overshadow you" (Luke 1:35). The glory of God was going to descend *into her womb* in the person of Jesus! And now the disciples are "overshadowed" by God's glory. But it has not come down from on high as it did when God descended to the tabernacle. It has just walked up the mountain alongside them. It is Jesus.

By revealing the glory of Christ's divinity through his humanity, the transfiguration also reveals the glory of Christ's humanity. God treasures the human body so much that in Christ he has taken human form to redeem the body. What Jesus experienced was a *union of divine and human natures*—unique to himself. But because of this unique union of natures, those who are in Christ by faith can experience a *union of relationship*. In Christ we connect with God.

So Jesus' humanity restores our humanity, and his trans-figuration prefigures our glorified humanity. Theologian Kathryn Tanner writes, "The Spirit radiates the humanity of Jesus with the Father's own gift of light, life and love; and shines through him, not simply back to the Father, but through his humanity to us, thereby communicating to us the gifts received by Jesus from the Father."[15]

We have no reason ever to despise our bodies and the life we live in them. Christ himself took a human body, and he has it still. And one day Christ will redeem and restore the bodies of his people—including yours.

MEDITATION

Today the Lord has truly appeared on the mountain;
today the old nature belonging to Adam—
once made in the image of God,
but dimmed to resemble the shapes of idols—
is transformed in shape once again,
transfigured to its ancient beauty in
God's image and likeness …
Today, on the mountain,
he … has put on a divinely-woven robe,
"wrapping himself in light as in a garment".

(The 7th-century abbot Anastasius of Sinai)[16]

THE
RADIANT
WORDS
OF JESUS

THE SECOND WEEK OF LENT

SUNDAY

It's not just the Gospel writers who recall the story of the transfiguration. Peter does so in his second letter. And remember: Peter was there!

For we did not follow cleverly devised stories when we told you about the coming of our Lord Jesus Christ in power, but we were eye-witnesses of his majesty. He received honour and glory from God the Father when the voice came to him from the Majestic Glory, saying, "This is my Son, whom I love; with him I am well pleased." We ourselves heard this voice that came from heaven when we were with him on the sacred mountain.

We also have the prophetic message as something completely reliable, and you will do well to pay attention to it, as to a light shining in a dark place, until the day dawns and the morning star rises in your hearts. Above all, you must understand that no prophecy of Scripture came about by the prophet's own interpretation of things. For prophecy never had its origin in the human will, but prophets, though human, spoke from God as they were carried along by the Holy Spirit.

(2 Peter 1:16-21)

Take time to read it through a couple of times, preferably aloud. First time round, read it at your normal pace. Second time round, read it slowly, savouring each phrase.

- *What do you find striking?*

- *What do you find odd?*

MONDAY

*For we did not follow cleverly devised
stories when we told you about the coming
of our Lord Jesus Christ in power.*

2 PETER 1:16

O ne of the oddest things about the transfiguration
is the words spoken by the voice from heaven:

*[Jesus] was transfigured before them. His clothes
became dazzling white, whiter than anyone in
the world could bleach them ... Then a cloud
appeared and covered them, and a voice came
from the cloud: "This is my Son, whom I love..."*
(Mark 9:2-3, 7)

What would you expect to come next? If you had
never read the story and it wasn't already familiar
to you, what would you expect? I suggest you might
expect the voice to say, *"Gaze upon him." Here is my
Son revealed in all his glory, his divinity shining though
his humanity, whiter than white. Look at him. Gaze
upon him. He's dazzling.*

Yet that's not what we read. God the Father says,
"Listen to him!" Why?

Here's one reason. It's a reason that speaks beyond Peter, James and John to the readers of Mark's Gospel— including us. For at this point you might be asking, "This is all well and good. But I can't see Jesus on a mountain. I can't see him at all. So how can I see his glory? You're telling me to contemplate the glory of the person of Christ... But how?"

The answer is: we see the glory of Christ in the gospel of Christ.

We don't get to see a vision of Jesus in the way Peter, James and John did. At least, not yet. But we can listen to the words of Jesus. The transfiguration is a confirmation that we can trust the message of Jesus.

This is how Peter himself sees it. In 2 Peter 1 he links his first-hand experience of the transfiguration with the authority and authenticity of the Bible. As we've seen, some people think the Bible contains only myths—fictional stories that express transcendent truths. Clearly some Bible stories are fictional tales told to proclaim spiritual truths—the parables of Jesus are the obvious examples. But these are clearly presented as fictional by the Bible itself. No one listening to Jesus would have imagined that his parables were historical accounts (though they may have been inspired by the everyday life he had observed growing up). When it comes to historical accounts, the Bible writers are intent on getting it right (Luke 1:3). Peter explicitly says, "We did not follow cleverly devised myths" (2 Peter 1:16 ESV).

We weren't there. But Peter gives us a reliable, first-hand account of what took place. He paints a picture so we can visualise it for ourselves.

Christians believe God can intervene in history and has done so supremely in the incarnation of his Son. Christianity is not simply a moral code or collection of religious insights. It's the declaration that God has conquered sin and death by acting in history through the life of Israel and through the incarnation of his Son.

What's interesting for our purposes is that Peter focuses on the transfiguration as his test case. Rather than rattle off a long list of all the miracles he saw—which could have included the healing of his own mother-in-law (Matthew 8:14-15) or his own experience of walking on water (14:28-31)—he zeros in on the transfiguration. Why this story?

One reason, as we've seen, is that in the transfiguration the divinity of Christ shines through. The miracles Peter saw were not simply the acts of a remarkable human being. After all, some of the prophets had performed mighty miracles. But all the parallels we can draw from the transfiguration are parallels to appearances of God. The Bible is not simply the story of human beings trying to reach up to God. The Bible is the story of God reaching down to rescue us. Peter knew that for sure because he had once stood on a mountain with God-in-Christ. Peter had seen the "majesty" (2 Peter 1:16) of God the Son, and he had heard the affirmation of that majesty by God the Father. The "majesty" of Jesus in verse 16 of his letter is matched by the "Majestic Glory" in verse 17: Jesus the Son is as majestic as God the Father.

Today we can't climb a mountain to see God. But we can see the majestic glory of God in the majesty of Christ, revealed in the pages of our Bibles.

MEDITATION

We have a sure prophetic Word
By inspiration of the Lord;
And though assailed on ev'ry hand,
Jehovah's Word shall ever stand …

Abiding, steadfast, firm, and sure,
The teachings of the Word endure.
Blest he who trusts this steadfast Word;
His anchor holds in Christ, the Lord.

(Emanuel Cronenwett)

TUESDAY

The LORD your God will raise up for
you a prophet like me from among
you, from your fellow Israelites.

DEUTERONOMY 18:15

There's a second reason why Peter zeros in on the transfiguration as he discusses the authority of the Bible: Jesus appeared on the mountain with Moses and Elijah. Together Moses and Elijah represent the law and the prophets—that is, the message of the Old Testament. Moses was the one through whom the old-covenant law was given, and Elijah was the archetypal prophet.

On the mountain there was a mutual affirmation of authority between the old and new covenants that works in both directions.

- *In one direction, Jesus affirms the authority of the Old Testament through the transfiguration (as we'll see in the next chapter).*

- *In the other direction, Moses and Elijah affirm that Jesus is the fulfilment of their testimony.*

This is the one of whom we spoke, Moses and Elijah are saying, by standing alongside Jesus. All the Old

Testament—law and prophecy—finds its endpoint in Jesus. He is its ultimate meaning. Moses and Elijah, says Calvin, are present to indicate "that the Law and the prophets had no other goal than Christ".[17]

Peter describes the location of the transfiguration as "the sacred mountain" (2 Peter 1:18). Up until that point, Jews would have thought of "the sacred mountain" as Mount Sinai. 1 Kings 19:8 calls Mount Sinai (or Mount Horeb, as it was also known) "the mountain of God". This was the place where Israel had met with God and where God had made a covenant with his people. Peter wants us to link these two events on two sacred mountains. God revealed himself through Moses on the Sacred Mountain 1.0 (Mount Sinai), and God revealed himself on the Sacred Mountain 2.0 (the mount of transfiguration). So if you accept the authority of the prophets in the Old Testament, then you should accept the authority of the apostles sent out by Jesus in the New Testament.

The words "listen to him" have another echo in the Old Testament story. Moses had said, "The LORD your God will raise up for you a prophet like me from among you, from your fellow Israelites" (Deuteronomy 18:15). How would they recognise this coming prophet? He would be "like me," said Moses. And what did Moses look like? The appearance of Moses is only ever described once, and that is in Exodus 34, when we're told that his face was radiant (Exodus 34:29). And now here is Jesus, and his face is radiant, shining like the sun. And Moses is standing next to him as if to say, *Here he is—the prophet I promised.*

Not only that but consider how Moses continues in Deuteronomy 18:15: "The Lord your God will raise up for you a prophet like me from among you, from your fellow Israelites. You *must listen to him*." This is exactly what the voice from the cloud says. When the voice of God says, "Listen to him", he is saying, *Jesus is the prophet promised by Moses; Jesus is the ultimate revelation of God, the eternal Word, the true Prophet.*

All the authority of the Old Testament—all its promises, all the moments of revelation it records—is funnelled into one point: Jesus. The authority Moses and Elijah received from Jesus, who is the Word of God, is reflected back to Jesus, as the Old Testament confirms him to be God's promised Saviour-King. In effect the voice from heaven is saying, *Listen to him, for Jesus is the fulfilment and embodiment of everything else I have ever said before.*

People sometimes pit the Old Testament against the New. They claim the God of the Old Testament is different from the God revealed by Jesus. But the Old and New Testaments speak with one voice, and that voice is Jesus!

MEDITATION

Father of mercies, in thy word,
What endless glory shines!
Forever be thy name adored
For these celestial lines.
Here the Redeemer's welcome voice
Spreads heavenly peace around;
And life and everlasting joys
Attend the blissful sound.
Here springs of consolation rise
To cheer the fainting mind,
And thirsty souls receive supplies
And sweet refreshment find.
O may these hallowed pages be
My ever dear delight.
And still new beauties may I see,
And still increasing light.

(The 18th-century hymn writer Anne Steele)

WEDNESDAY

*"I have not come to abolish [the Law and
the Prophets] but to fulfil them."*

MATTHEW 5:17

We've seen how the appearance of Moses and Elijah at the transfiguration shows that the Old Testament affirms Jesus as its fulfilment. But the opposite is also true: at the transfiguration *Jesus affirms the authority of the Old Testament.*

By standing alongside Moses and Elijah, Jesus confirms their testimony. The Old Testament is to be trusted because it was trusted and affirmed by Jesus, the Son of God. When God himself comes to earth, he teaches the Scriptures. Jesus always quoted those Scriptures as reliable and authoritative. Even when he says, "You have heard it said… but I tell you…" (Matthew 5:21-22, 27-28, 31-32, 33-34, 38-39, 43-44), he wasn't repudiating the Old Testament but going further and deeper. Indeed, in the same context Jesus says, "Do not think that I have come to abolish the Law or the Prophets; I have not come to abolish them but to fulfil them" (v 17).

Peter makes the same point. "We also have the prophetic message as something completely reliable," he says in 2 Peter 1:19. God reveals himself and his purposes through his actions in history—rescuing Israel and sending Jesus. But God goes further. He also ensures we have an accurate record of those events and an accurate interpretation of those events. "No prophecy of Scripture came about by the prophet's own interpretation of things," says verse 20. The Scriptures never simply present a human viewpoint. Yes, the human writers leave something of their own personalities on the pages of Scripture. But Peter says, "Prophecy never had its origin in the human will, but prophets, though human, spoke from God as they were carried along by the Holy Spirit" (v 21). God himself, through his Holy Spirit, ensured the accuracy of what they wrote. The result is "something completely reliable" (v 19).

What Peter literally says in this verse is that we have the prophetic word made firmer. The Old Testament was already firm because it came from God. But now it has been made firmer by its fulfilment in Christ—"confirmed" we might say.

Suppose I promise to write a book by the end of May. That's not a hypothetical scenario as that's the deadline for this book! My publishers may consider this a firm promise because they trust me to deliver on time. But if and when the manuscript lands in their email inbox, then they might say my promise has been *confirmed*. The Scriptures were "something completely reliable" before Jesus came. Now that reliability has been *confirmed* by their fulfilment in Christ.

For Peter, the transfiguration is his go-to proof of the reliability of Scripture—including both the Old and New Testaments. We can trust the message of Jesus in the New Testament because the person of Jesus was affirmed by the transfiguration. We can trust the past promises of Jesus in the Old Testament because the promises of God were affirmed and confirmed by the transfiguration. And we can trust the transfiguration itself because Peter, James and John were eye-witnesses of what happened.

Every way you look at it, you can trust the words you read in your Bible. They are the words of God. "Listen to him."

MEDITATION

"For you have been born again,
not of perishable seed, but of imperishable,
through the living and enduring word of God.
For, 'All people are like grass,
and all their glory is like the flowers of the field;
the grass withers and the flowers fall,
but the word of the Lord endures for ever.'
And this is the word that was preached to you."

(1 Peter 1:23-25 and Isaiah 40:6-8)

THURSDAY

"I am the Root and the Offspring of David,
and the bright Morning Star."

REVELATION 22:16

A reliable account of the story of Jesus is important. It means I can trust what I read. But how does that bring me any nearer to seeing the glory of Jesus for myself? It's great to have an accurate record of the disciples seeing Christ's glory. But that's still only a second-hand encounter. Can we go one better?

Consider again what Peter says in 2 Peter 1:19: "We also have the prophetic message as something completely reliable, and you will do well to pay attention to it, as to a light shining in a dark place, until the day dawns and the morning star rises in your hearts". Peter speaks of a coming day when the morning star will rise in our hearts. In Revelation 22:16 Jesus identifies himself as the "morning star". A day is coming when Jesus will light up the world with his glory—just as he did in miniature at the transfiguration.

In the meantime, that light shines through the pages of the Bible—even now as "a light shining in a dark place" (2 Peter 1:19). This is where we see the glory of Christ. Paul develops this idea:

The god of this age has blinded the minds of
unbelievers, so that they cannot see the light of the
gospel that displays the glory of Christ, who is the
image of God. For what we preach is not ourselves,
but Jesus Christ as Lord, and ourselves as your
servants for Jesus' sake. For God, who said, "Let
light shine out of darkness," made his light shine
in our hearts to give us the light of the knowledge
of God's glory displayed in the face of Christ.
(2 Corinthians 4:4-6)

How do we see the glory of God? Verse 6 says, "For God, who said, 'Let light shine out of darkness,' made his light shine in our hearts to give us the light of the knowledge of God's glory displayed in the face of Christ". We see the glory of God in the glory of Christ. Except, of course, that in verse 6 Paul says, "the *face* of Christ". Perhaps that's because Paul is alluding to the transfiguration, when the *face* of Christ "shone like the sun" (Matthew 17:2).

So we see the glory of God in the glory of Christ. But how do we see the glory of Christ? Paul speaks of "the light of the gospel that displays the glory of Christ" (2 Corinthians 4:4). What reveals the glory of Christ is "the light of the gospel". You probably know this from your experience. Perhaps you've read your Bible and have been overwhelmed by the amazing grace of Christ. Or you've listened to the word being preached and have been blown away by the glory of Christ. Yet even when we don't *feel* anything, God is still illuminating our hearts through his word.

This was Moses' experience back in Exodus 33 – 34. The previous chapter of 2 Corinthians has explored the way the face of Moses radiated after he saw (albeit only partially) the glory of God. Except that the text of Exodus 34 doesn't say the face of Moses was radiating after seeing God. What it actually says is that it was "because he had *spoken* with the LORD" (v 29). It is the word of God that reveals the glory of God.

It was the same for Elijah. God was not present in the wind or the earthquake or the fire (1 Kings 19:12). But he revealed his presence to Elijah through "a gentle whisper"—the voice of his word.

Why read the Bible day by day? Because we meet Jesus in its pages. Through the Holy Spirit, we see his glory and hear his voice.

MEDITATION

See whose glory fills the skies:
Jesus, the light of the world!
Sun of righteousness, arise:
Jesus, the light of the world!

Pierce the gloom of sin and grief,
Jesus, the light of the world!
Scatter all my unbelief,
Jesus, the light of the world!

More and more thyself display,
Jesus, the light of the world!
Shining to the perfect day,
Jesus, the light of the world!

Visit, then, this soul of mine,
Jesus, light of the world!
Fill me, Radiancy divine!
Jesus, the light of the world!

(Charles Wesley)

FRIDAY

*They saw that his face was like
the face of an angel.*

ACTS 6:15

Jesus does more than affirm the Old Testament; he *completes* it.

"When Moses went up on the mountain," says Exodus 24:15-16, "the cloud covered it, and the glory of the LORD settled on Mount Sinai". We're told that the cloud covered the mountain for six days, and then on the seventh day, "the LORD called to Moses from within the cloud" (v 16). So cloud descended on a mountain when Moses received the old-covenant law. Now at the transfiguration, cloud again descends on a mountain (with Moses present) to confirm that the message of Jesus represents a new "law" with a new covenant—the fulfilment of the old covenant. As Moses and Elijah are caught up in the glory of Christ, it's as if the Old Testament is transfigured alongside Jesus or in the radiance of Jesus. The inner luminescence of its words is made manifest in and through the coming of Christ.

What does this say about the way we should read the Old Testament? Its words are transfigured in Jesus. All the partial fulfilments of God's promises in the institutions of Israel's religion or the heroes of Israel's history pointed forward to a fuller fulfilment in Christ. So we can and should expect to see Jesus on every page of the Old Testament.

There's a lovely little parallel between the story of Moses and the story of Stephen, the first Christian martyr. Stephen is hauled in front of the Sanhedrin, accused of speaking "blasphemous words against Moses and against God" (Acts 6:11). As Stephen stands there, even before he has spoken, we read, "All who were sitting in the Sanhedrin looked intently at Stephen, and they saw that his face was like the face of an angel" (v 15). It's an echo of the face of Moses being radiant after hearing God's voice in Exodus 34:29—even though Stephen has just been accused of speaking "against Moses". But, instead of being "against Moses", Stephen is *like* Moses. Like Moses and like Jesus. For at the transfiguration the face of Jesus also shone (Matthew 17:2).

And what is Stephen's message? That the Law and the Prophets have found their fulfilment in Jesus of Nazareth. He reveals their true meaning. They are illuminated and become radiant as the face of Jesus is illuminated and becomes radiant. Stephen is about to preach this and, as he does so, his face also shines like that of an angel.

The transfiguration teaches us how to read the Old Testament. Moses and Elijah turn up to see the fulfilment of everything they had done and said. And they teach us to do the same: to see the fulfilment of their words in Jesus. Praise him that we have the wisdom and comfort of God's truth available to us today.

MEDITATION

*"The pages of both covenants corroborate
each other,
and he whom under the veil of mysteries
the types that went before had promised,
is displayed clearly and conspicuously
by the splendour of the present glory."*

*(The 5th-century theologian and pope
Leo the Great)*[18]

SATURDAY

*We also have the prophetic message as
something completely reliable.*

2 PETER 1:19

We've seen how, in the transfiguration, Jesus affirms the authority of the Old Testament, and in the transfiguration, the Old Testament (represented by Moses and Elijah) affirms the authority of Jesus. All the promises of the Old Testament find their "Yes" in Jesus (2 Corinthians 1:20). The whole Bible is a reliable account of the message of Jesus.

So what?

Here's Peter's own application of this truth: "We also have the prophetic message as something completely reliable, and you will do well to *pay attention* to it" (2 Peter 1:19). All the weight of God is behind the Scriptures: Old Testament and New Testament. This is God's word to you. So it's a good idea to pay attention to what it says! We're not just reading the writings of a human being; we're hearing the very words of God. When we talk about paying attention to Scripture, what we're really talking about is *paying attention* to God as he has revealed himself in Scripture.

Paying attention means listening attentively. Who's against that? No one. But we're so easily distracted when we read God's word.

Sometimes when I'm driving on the motorway or freeway, I suddenly realise that I can't remember overtaking any cars or being overtaken. The road is straight, and my speed is constant, so it's as if I've switched over to autopilot. I'm not paying attention to what's going on around me.

I can do something similar when I'm reading my Bible. I sometimes finish my allotted reading for the day, only to realise I can't really remember anything much of what I've read. And I normally read the Bible out loud! I've been reading on autopilot—without paying attention. Or I can listen to a sermon and find I've zoned out, until the preacher raises his voice or drops his Bible. But these words are the message of Jesus, the Word of God. And God says to us—as he said to Peter, James and John—"Listen to him" (Mark 9:7). Pay attention with your full attention.

But paying attention means more than simply listening carefully. It also involves obeying what we hear.

Suppose a mother tells her son to tidy his bedroom. In this situation, paying attention means a whole lot more for the boy than simply reflecting on his mother's words. If he's failed to tidy his room, then she'll not be impressed, even if he can recall what she said word for word. What paying attention means for him is straightforward: it means doing what she's said.

In the same way, the word of Jesus conveys more than just information. It demands a response—a response of faith or obedience or love or worship.

How has God been speaking to you through his word recently—perhaps through the preaching of your church or through the reading this book? What might it mean for you to "pay attention"?

MEDITATION

O Word of God incarnate,
O Wisdom from on high,
O Truth unchanged, unchanging,
O Light of our dark sky:
We praise you for the radiance
That from the hallowed page –
A lantern to our footsteps –
Shines on from age to age.

(William Walsham How)

THE
RADIANT
LOVE OF
JESUS

SUNDAY

We've looked at the account of the transfiguration in Mark's Gospel, along with Peter's reflections on it in 2 Peter 1. It's time to move out and consider how the story of the transfiguration sits in the wider landscape of Mark's Gospel.

> *Jesus and his disciples went on to the villages around Caesarea Philippi. On the way he asked them, "Who do people say I am?"*
>
> *They replied, "Some say John the Baptist; others say Elijah; and still others, one of the prophets."*
>
> *"But what about you?" he asked. "Who do you say I am?"*
>
> *Peter answered, "You are the Messiah."*
>
> *Jesus warned them not to tell anyone about him.*

He then began to teach them that the Son of Man must suffer many things and be rejected by the elders, the chief priests and the teachers of the law, and that he must be killed and after three days rise again. He spoke plainly about this, and Peter took him aside and began to rebuke him.

But when Jesus turned and looked at his disciples, he rebuked Peter. "Get behind me, Satan!" he said. "You do not have in mind the concerns of God, but merely human concerns."

Then he called the crowd to him along with his disciples and said: "Whoever wants to be my disciple must deny themselves and take up their cross and follow me. For whoever wants to save their life will lose it, but whoever loses their life for me and for the gospel will save it. What good is it for someone to gain the whole world, yet forfeit their soul? Or what can anyone give in exchange for their soul? If anyone is ashamed of me and my words in this adulterous and sinful generation, the Son of Man will be ashamed of them when he comes in his Father's glory with the holy angels."

And he said to them, "Truly I tell you, some who are standing here will not taste death before they see that the kingdom of God has come with power."

After six days Jesus took Peter, James and John with him and led them up a high mountain, where they were all alone. There he was transfigured before them. His clothes became dazzling white, whiter than anyone in the world could bleach them. And there appeared before them Elijah and Moses, who were talking with Jesus.

Peter said to Jesus, "Rabbi, it is good for us to be here. Let us put up three shelters—one for you, one for Moses and one for Elijah." (He did not know what to say, they were so frightened.)

Then a cloud appeared and covered them, and a voice came from the cloud: "This is my Son, whom I love. Listen to him!"

(Mark 8:27 – 9:7)

Take time to read this passage through a couple of times, preferably aloud. First time round, read it at your normal pace. Second time round, read it slowly, savouring each phrase.

- *How does this wider context explain why the voice from the cloud said, "Listen to him" (v 7)? Consider what Jesus has just said and how the disciples have reacted.*

MONDAY

"But what about you?" he asked.
"Who do you say I am?"

MARK 8:29

We recently had an issue with our plumbing. "No problem," I thought. My friend Bob was coming round, and Bob's an engineer. "He'll know what to do," I told myself. It turns out that understanding fluid dynamics is not the same as being able to fix a leaking radiator. My expectations of engineers were sadly mistaken.

Peter has just confessed Jesus to be the Messiah, God's promised Saviour-King. And Jesus has begun to revolutionise the mistaken expectations of the disciples. One purpose of the transfiguration is to reinforce that process of re-education. The issue at stake is this: what kind of a messiah is the Messiah? What kind of king?

The voice from heaven is heard not once but twice in Mark's Gospel—at the baptism of Jesus at the beginning of the *first* half of the Gospel and here at the transfiguration at the beginning of the *second* half of the Gospel. In both cases the voice of God the Father begins with the words "This is my Son". It's not simply a reference to Jesus being the eternal Son of God, the second Person of the Trinity. It's also an allusion to the covenant with King David in 2 Samuel 7, which is celebrated in Psalm 2:7: "I will proclaim the Lord's decree: He said to me, 'You are my son; today I have become your father.'" The kings of Israel were adopted by God as his quasi-sons, as a sign of their divine authority.

At the transfiguration, God himself quotes these words and applies them to Jesus: Jesus is the promised messianic King. Except that Jesus is no quasi-son; he's the real thing. He's both the promised son of David *and* the divine Son of God.

Mark's Gospel begins, "The beginning of the good news about Jesus the Messiah, the Son of God". This story is going to be good news, and the good news is that Jesus is the promised Messiah and Jesus is the Son of God. That double declaration forms the structure of the book as a whole. The first half of Mark's Gospel comes to a climax with Peter's confession, in Mark 8:29: that Jesus is the Messiah. The first half of the Gospel asks the question "Who is this?" and the answer it gives is "You are the Messiah" (4:41; 8:29).

The second half of the Gospel comes to a climax with the confession of the centurion at the cross: that Jesus is the Son of God. But this realisation came when the centurion "saw how he died" (15:39). God is known through the cross. The first half of Mark's Gospel is full of miracles—all revealing the authority of Jesus as God's Messiah. In the second half, the miracles are replaced with a discussion of what it means to follow Jesus (chapters 9 – 10) and the story of his Passion (chapters 11 – 16). In other words, it's the cross which dominates the second half of the Gospel.

What kind of a messiah is the Messiah? What kind of king? A king who dies a horrible death!

So Mark begins the second half of his Gospel with Jesus predicting his death: "He then began to teach them that the Son of Man must suffer many things and be rejected by the elders, the chief priests and the teachers of the law, and that he must be killed and after three days rise again" (8:31). Now that the disciples have recognised him as the Messiah, Jesus can begin to teach them what it means for him to be the Messiah—that the Messiah must suffer and die.

This is the glory of our King's love: he has come to suffer for his people. His glory consists not just in his extraordinary power but also in his amazing love.

MEDITATION

O sacred Head once wounded,
With grief and shame weighed down.
How scornfully surrounded
With thorns, thine only crown!
Thy grief and thy compassion
Were all for sinners' gain:
Mine, mine was the transgression,
But thine the deadly pain.

(Paulus Gerhardt, trans. James W. Alexander)

TUESDAY

He then began to teach them that the
Son of Man must suffer many things.

MARK 8:31

Sometimes we urge someone to listen because they've not heard what's being said. But sometimes we urge someone to listen because they've *rejected* what's being said. There's no problem with their hearing, or even with their comprehension. They've understood perfectly well but chosen to reject what they've been told. Perhaps this is why the voice from heaven says, "Listen".

The divine call to listen reinforces the importance of listening to Jesus in his word, the Bible, especially as it's combined with the presence of Moses and Elijah, the representatives of the old-covenant teachings. But this only takes us halfway to understanding why the voice says, "Listen to him". Something more is going on. God the Father is not simply exhorting the disciples to listen to the word of Christ in general; he has a specific word in mind.

When Jesus first predicts his death, Peter is appalled and rebukes him (Mark 8:31-33). The Jews expected the Messiah to come in glory and triumph. After all, he was God's anointed King, the liberator. They expected him to sweep away God's enemies. Peter is appalled at the thought that Jesus might be less than this. What he needs to realise is that Jesus is going to be much, much *more*.

Already, in the parables of Mark 4, Jesus has said the kingdom comes secretly. Yes, one day God's kingdom will come in power (as Peter demanded). This future coming will establish justice through judgment. But *first* the kingdom comes secretly. First the Messiah must suffer and die. The problem with the coming in power is that we're all God's enemies. If the kingdom comes in conquest, then we're all in the firing line. But God's plan is to save his people, to create a new humanity and to grant forgiveness. So first Christ must die in our place. The King himself is going to be conquered. He is going to bear our punishment. This is why, in the second part of Mark's Gospel, Jesus resolutely heads towards Jerusalem: he is on the way to the cross.

Peter realises none of this. He will. Later the idea will so captivate him that he will keep coming back to it in his writings (1 Peter 1:18-19; 2:21-25; 3:18). But for now, he wants glory without suffering. Along with the other disciples, he wants the power, wealth and prestige of being part of the King's entourage. So Peter is outraged by the words of Jesus. Peter is right to name Jesus as the Messiah, but at this point Peter has no idea what it really means for Jesus to be the Messiah.

This then is why the voice from heaven says, "Listen to him." It's because Peter has just refused to listen to Jesus (Mark 8:33). God is saying in effect, *Listen to Jesus when he speaks of the cross. He has not misunderstood the mission of the Messiah. This is exactly what my Son and I agreed together before the foundation of the world. His determination to head to the cross is the climax of our eternal plan to display our love and redeem a people.*

So "listen to him" means more than listening to Jesus' words in general (important as that is). It specifically includes listening to what he says about the cross. Again, the presence of Moses and Elijah reinforces the challenge of the cross. They represent the Old Testament, and their presence reminds us that the idea of a suffering Messiah is not new (1 Peter 1:10-11). It is the fulfilment of what God had promised.

Still today people try to embrace Jesus without the cross. They want Jesus as a model but not as a Saviour. They treat the cross as an example of love but not as a sacrifice for sin. But Jesus said, "The Son of Man *must* suffer many things" (Mark 8:31). His life *must* end with crucifixion. Jesus says this, and then the Father says, "Listen to him". For all its visual impact, the challenge of the transfiguration is to not be ashamed of the message of the *cross*.

This is the glory of our King's love: he is *determined* to suffer for his people.

MEDITATION

Jesus says:
*"If anyone is ashamed of me and my words
in this adulterous and sinful generation,
the Son of Man will be ashamed of them
when he comes in his Father's glory with
the holy angels."*

(Mark 8:38)

Paul says:
*"I am not ashamed of the gospel,
because it is the power of God that brings
salvation to everyone who believes:
first to the Jew, then to the Gentile."*

(Romans 1:16)

WEDNESDAY

But when Jesus turned and looked at
his disciples, he rebuked Peter.

MARK 8:33

Jesus hears the voice of Satan in the words of Peter. Satan's temptation of Jesus is unwittingly renewed by Peter. As Jesus embraces the horror of the cross by taking the road to Jerusalem, Satan comes to suggest there might be another way: the crown without the cross. Satan offers Jesus all the glory with none of the agony. You can see the appeal. But it would have involved Jesus abandoning his people. If Jesus doesn't die for his people, then they will perish. He might be acclaimed as King, but his people would be lost for ever. Any glory he received would be empty. If there was another way, then Jesus would take it, but he must head for the cross.

The 6th-century presbyter Leontius has a powerful sermon in which he imaginatively elaborates the response of Jesus to Peter:[19]

> *"You are a stumbling block to me," Peter, "because*
> *you are not thinking the things of God, but those*

of human beings." (Matthew 16:23) If I am not put to death, none of you will taste immortality.

"You are a stumbling block to me," Peter. If I am not murdered, none of you will inherit the vineyard. (Matthew 21:38)

"You are a stumbling-block to me," Peter. "For you are not thinking the things of God, but those of human beings." I am "the grain of wheat" ... [and] "unless the grain of wheat falls into the ground and dies, it remains alone. But if it dies, it produces much fruit." (John 12:24)

"You are a stumbling block to me," Peter, "because you are not thinking the things of God but those of human beings." If I do not go down to the underworld, no one will set Adam free from slavery.

"You are a stumbling block to me," Peter, "because you are not thinking the things of God, but of human beings." If I am not sacrificed, no one will bestow on you a mystical reward. If I am not crucified, Peter, the thief will not enter an open Paradise.

"You are a stumbling block to me," Peter, "because you are not thinking the things of God, but of human beings." I came not only to protect the living, but to benefit those who are fallen asleep.

I did not deceive you, then, Peter, when I said, "I am the light" and "the resurrection and the life." (John 8:12; 12:25) Since I am light, Peter, I must "shine on those in darkness." (Luke 1:79) What kind of light does not put darkness to flight?

"I am the resurrection," Peter. I must raise up those who have already overcome. For what kind of resurrection is it that does not raise those fallen asleep?

"I am the life," Peter. I must put death to death; for I suffer as a human, and I save as a lover of humanity.

Now I suffer according to the divine plan, Peter. But not long from now I will come as divine Lord: not showing myself in the form of a servant (Philippians 2:7), but led in triumphal procession by angels, in the glory of my Father. (Matthew 16:27) Now I allow myself to be rejected, through the ordinariness of what people see, but after a little while I will judge with authority, through the power of God.

MEDITATION

Who is he in yonder stall,
At whose feet the shepherds fall?
Who is he in deep distress,
Fasting in the wilderness?
Who is he upon the tree
Dies in shame and agony?
Who is he that from the grave
Comes to heal and help and save?
'Tis the Lord, O wondrous story!
'Tis the Lord, the King of glory!
At his feet we humbly fall,
Crown him, crown him, Lord of all!

(Benjamin R. Hanby)

THURSDAY

*"Whoever wants to be my disciple must deny
themselves and take up their cross and follow me."*

MARK 8:34

66 ❙ t's time for bed." "But Dad, I just need to finish
this." Children are experts at procrastination. As
bedtime approaches, they remember some unfinished
homework that must be done, or they clean their teeth
with uncharacteristic thoroughness. I wonder what you
as an adult do to put off what you don't enjoy. We see
Peter doing this at the transfiguration. Jesus is resolutely heading to Jerusalem to face the cross, and Peter
wants to slow things down.

Jesus is not simply our example; first and foremost, he
is our Saviour. And the cross is not simply a display of
love; first and foremost, it's a sacrifice for sin. We must
start with God's grace to us in Christ. But the cross is
also to be the pattern for those saved by its power.

After predicting his sufferings, Jesus said to his disciples, "Whoever wants to be my disciple must deny
themselves and take up their cross and follow me"
(Mark 8:34). The following chapters in Mark's Gospel
are an explanation of what it means to walk the way of

the cross. Three times in Mark 8 – 10 Jesus predicts his death, and each time he follows that by teaching what it means to follow a suffering Messiah. Self-denial, sacrificial love and submission to God are the marks of those who follow Jesus, and nowhere are these marks more clearly seen than at Calvary. As Jesus teaches his disciples about the way *of* the cross, he is demonstrating it to them as he journeys on his way *to* the cross.

This may be one reason—perhaps even the primary reason—why Peter suggests building shelters. He wants glory, and he does not want the cross. So, when he encounters glory, he wants to pin it down and make it permanent. He tries to procrastinate—to delay the journey to the cross. A sermon by a deacon named Pantoleon, possibly from the 6th century, says, "Since [Peter] was not able to prevent the Passion, he schemes to postpone the journey to Jerusalem, not by saying openly what he desires, but lobbying Jesus that by being here, they might not depart for there".[20]

In another early sermon, Timothy of Antioch imagines the response of Jesus to Peter's suggestion: "What are you thinking of, Peter? … Shall I obey your will, or shall I save the world? Shall I remain here? And who will raise Adam from his sleep? Who will set Eve free? Who will redeem the world? Do you care only for yourself, but nothing for the whole universe?"[21]

If fact, Jesus himself makes no response. Instead, it is the voice from heaven which responds to this request by telling Peter to listen to the message of the cross. When the Father says, "Listen to him", he's not simply calling us to embrace the crucified King; he's also calling us to embrace the crucified *life*—a life in which we die to self and live to serve others.

What might it mean for you today to deny yourself, take up your cross and follow Jesus? Are there acts of sacrificial love and service that are you postponing? Listen to Jesus, and follow him on the way of the cross, for it leads to glory.

MEDITATION

Jesus says:
"For whoever wants to save their life will lose it, but whoever loses their life for me and for the gospel will save it."

(Mark 8:35)

FRIDAY

*"No one takes [my life] from me, but
I lay it down of my own accord."*

JOHN 10:18

Yesterday we were called to embrace the way of the cross. But that's tough. In Roman times the cross was a symbol of utmost shame. Not much has changed. The cross is still viewed with contempt. And accepting the self-denial and service of the way of the cross is tough. What can help us to remain faithful when our path is hard? We need a vision of glory.

One of the oldest-recorded sermons on the transfiguration (we quoted from it yesterday) is attributed to Timothy of Antioch, a figure about whom we know nothing else. Timothy says Christ "did not leave his disciples swimming in the tidal wave of unbelief" but revealed his glory at the transfiguration "so that the disciples might remain steadfast, supported by what they saw and heard".[22] In other words, Peter, James and John were given the opportunity to see Jesus transfigured so they would not lose heart when they saw Jesus crucified.

It's an idea echoed by the church father Leo the Great: "In this transfiguration the foremost object was to remove the offence of the cross from the disciple's heart, and to prevent their faith being disturbed by the humiliation of His voluntary Passion by revealing to them the excellence of His hidden dignity".[23]

We find the same idea in the 17th-century Puritan Thomas Manton: "For the confirmation of their faith, Christ would give his disciples a glimpse of his glory; he knew they would be sorely assaulted and shaken by the ignominy of his cross".[24] Jesus did not want his disciples to be "mentally overwhelmed" when they witnessed the crucifixion.[25]

The glory of Jesus at the transfiguration reminds us that Jesus chose the path that leads to the cross. It wasn't forced upon him. The one who was so gloriously transfigured clearly had the power to resist his arrest or come down from the cross if he had chosen to do so. But in love he chose to remain so he could die in our place. "I lay down my life for the sheep ... No one takes it from me, but I lay it down of my own accord" (John 10:15, 18).

The glory of Jesus at the transfiguration also reminds us of the *purpose* of the cross. Jesus died that we might be forgiven, and we are forgiven that we might share the glory of Jesus. Speaking of "those who will believe in me", Jesus prays to his Father: "Father, I want those you have given me to be with me where I am, and to see my glory, the glory you have given me because you loved me before the creation of the world" (17:24).

The words of Timothy of Antioch, Leo the Great and Thomas Manton are words to us today.

When *the message of the cross* is derided or attacked, the transfiguration encourages us not to be ashamed of its offence. The one who dies in weakness is the one whose glory we see on the mountain. Salvation through substitution is the way Jesus chose to establish his kingdom.

And when we draw back from *the way of the cross*, the glimpse of Jesus' radiance at the transfiguration reminds us that this is the way to glory.

We ended yesterday by asking ourselves: what might it mean for us today to deny ourselves, take up our cross and follow Jesus? Today we must add: what might it mean for us today to set our sights on the glory of Jesus?

MEDITATION

"I consider that our present sufferings are not worth comparing with the glory that will be revealed in us."

(Romans 8:18)

SATURDAY

*After he said this, he was taken up before their
very eyes, and a cloud hid him from their sight.*

ACTS 1:9

What do you do when you sin? Christians know
they've been forgiven their past, present and future sins. But when we sin, it's hard not to feel that
a question mark hangs over us as far as God is concerned. So what should we do? One answer is: *look up.*

We've looked back in the Bible story to explore precedents for the transfiguration. It's time to look *forward*
to an important parallel: the ascension of Jesus. At the
transfiguration Jesus ascends a mountain to be covered
by a cloud; and at the ascension he ascends into the sky
to be hidden in a cloud (Acts 1:9).

The prophet Daniel has a dream that helps us make
sense of the ascension (Daniel 7:9-14). While the disciples observe the ascension from below, Daniel is shown a
preview of the ascension *from above.* Daniel sees the son
of man come "with the clouds of heaven" (v 13) before
the Ancient of Days. He sees, as it were, what happens
on the other side.

In Daniel's vision it becomes clear that the ascension is *a victory parade*. Jesus came to earth, took on sin at the cross, wrestled with death in the grave, and rose in triumph. Now he returns to heaven as the victor. Jesus ascends into heaven to be given all authority (Matthew 28:18). He is the conqueror, and the worship of the nations is his prize. "There before me," says Daniel, "was one like a son of man, coming with the clouds of heaven. He approached the Ancient of Days and was led into his presence. He was given authority, glory and sovereign power; all nations and peoples of every language worshipped him" (Daniel 7:13-14).

Jesus has suffered: the bite of the whip and the pain of the nails, mockery from his enemies and desertion by his friends. And darkest of all, he has borne the wrath of his Father as he died in our place. But now... now he enters heaven to the cheers of the angels. And Psalm 24 tells us what they sing as Jesus arrives:

> *Lift up your heads, you gates;*
> * be lifted up, you ancient doors,*
> *   that the King of glory may come in.*
>
> *Who is this King of glory?*
> * The LORD strong and mighty,*
> *   the LORD mighty in battle. (v 7-8)*

The ascension not only declares the victory of Jesus; it also declares his *vindication*. The place to which Jesus ascends is actually a courtroom: "The court was seated, and the books were opened," says Daniel 7:10. The verdict of the world—that Jesus was a blasphemer and troublemaker—is about to be overturned in the heavenly court of appeal.

Jesus doesn't just ascend into heaven on his own account; he comes as the representative of his people. What happens next? Jesus is declared to be in the right or righteous. And that verdict is our verdict. The life he lived, he lived on our behalf so that his obedience might be our obedience. The death he died, he died on our behalf so that the penalty of our sin might be paid in full. And the verdict he has received, he has received on our behalf so that we might be declared right in God's sight. God has appointed Jesus to be our advocate in heaven. Every sin we commit would throw our salvation into question were it not for the fact that Jesus intercedes on our behalf.

At the ascension Jesus became the first human being ever to enter heaven. And he paves the way for his people to follow. One day we, too, will ascend into the presence of God. Even now we can follow Jesus by faith.

Like the disciples ascending the mount of transfiguration to see the glory of Christ, we can look up by faith to see the victory of the ascended Jesus. Like the disciples looking up at the ascension, we can look up with faith to see Jesus in heaven on our behalf (Colossians 3:1). When sin accuses us, we can look up and see our "advocate with the Father—Jesus Christ, the Righteous One" (1 John 2:1).

MEDITATION

Before the throne of God above
I have a strong and perfect plea,
A great High Priest whose name is love,
Who ever lives and pleads for me.
My name is graven on His hands;
My name is written on His heart.
I know that while in heav'n he stands
No tongue can bid me thence depart.

When Satan tempts me to despair
And tells me of the guilt within,
Upward I look and see him there
Who made an end to all my sin.
Because the sinless Saviour died,
My sinful soul is counted free,
For God the Just is satisfied
To look on him and pardon me.

(Charitie Lees Bancroft, 1841-1892)

THE
RADIANT
PASSION
OF JESUS

THE FOURTH WEEK OF LENT

SUNDAY

We've looked at how Mark presents the story of the transfiguration. This week we turn to Luke's account. Luke tells the same story, but he tells it in his own distinctive way. There are parallels and patterns that Luke wants to spotlight.

The transfiguration took place on an unnamed mountain. Traditionally this has been identified as Mount Tabor. But modern scholars think this unlikely, partly because Tabor had a settlement on its summit. Wherever this mountain was, the distinctive way in which Luke tells the story links it to three other mountains: Mount Sinai, the Mount of Olives and the hill of Calvary. Luke gives us *a tale of four mountains.*

About eight days after Jesus said this, he took Peter, John and James with him and went up onto a mountain to pray. As he was praying, the appearance of his face changed, and his clothes became as bright as a flash of lightning. Two men, Moses and

*Elijah, appeared in glorious splendour, talking
with Jesus. They spoke about his departure, which
he was about to bring to fulfilment at Jerusalem.
Peter and his companions were very sleepy, but
when they became fully awake, they saw his glory
and the two men standing with him. As the men
were leaving Jesus, Peter said to him, "Master,
it is good for us to be here. Let us put up three
shelters—one for you, one for Moses and one for
Elijah." (He did not know what he was saying.)*

*While he was speaking, a cloud appeared and
covered them, and they were afraid as they entered
the cloud. A voice came from the cloud, saying,
"This is my Son, whom I have chosen; listen to
him." When the voice had spoken, they found that
Jesus was alone. The disciples kept this to themselves and did not tell anyone at that time what
they had seen.*

(Luke 9:28-36)

Take time to read it through a couple of times, preferably aloud. First time round, read it at your normal pace.
Second time round, read it slowly, savouring each phrase.

• *How does Luke's account differ from Mark's?*

MONDAY

*While he was speaking, a cloud appeared
and covered them, and they were
afraid as they entered the cloud.*

LUKE 9:34

Here are some of the distinctive features of Luke's presentation of the transfiguration:

- *Luke changes six days to eight days (we'll come back to that).*

- *Luke adds two references to prayer.*

- *Luke leaves out the word "transfigured" and adds a reference to lightning.*

- *Luke tells us what Jesus, Moses and Elijah were talking about.*

- *Luke adds a reference to Peter, James and John being sleepy.*

- *Luke links the fear of the disciples to being covered by the cloud.*

- *Luke speaks of them "entering" the cloud as being covered by it.*

- *Luke records the voice from heaven saying, "whom I have chosen" instead of "whom I love".*

Luke adds a reference to lightning and links the fear of the disciples to entering the cloud. Together these heighten the parallels to the story of God meeting his people at Mount Sinai. Lightning was a key feature at Sinai (Exodus 19:16). The same is true of the cloud:

> *When Moses went up on the mountain, the **cloud** covered it, and the glory of the LORD settled on Mount Sinai. For six days the **cloud** covered the mountain, and on the seventh day the LORD called to Moses from within the **cloud**. To the Israelites the glory of the LORD looked like a consuming fire on top of the mountain. Then Moses entered the **cloud** as he went on up the mountain.*
>
> *(Exodus 24:15-18)*

Mount Sinai was covered in cloud—as was the mount of transfiguration. Moses entered the cloud—as the disciples did on the mount of transfiguration. The Lord spoke from the cloud—as he does on the mount of transfiguration. And at Sinai the combination of lightning and cloud (or "smoke") lead to fear (Exodus 20:18)—as they do on the mount of transfiguration.

The experience of meeting with God at Mount Sinai was perpetuated in the tabernacle. That was the reason why the tabernacle was built. What took place at Mount Sinai was replicated in symbolic form in the tabernacle.

Let's focus on one aspect of this. In front of the tabernacle's Most Holy Place was the altar of incense. It was about a metre (3.3') high and half a metre (1.6') wide and deep—the size of a lectern. That's too small for sacrificing animals; all the sacrifices took place outside in the courtyard. Instead, the altar of incense produced a continual cloud of incense to surround the Most Holy Place. In so doing, it replicated and perpetuated the cloud that had covered Mount Sinai. So to enter the cloud of incense was to enter the Most Holy Place—just as Moses had entered the cloud to meet with God on Mount Sinai. Only the high priest could do that and only once a year through the sacrifice of atonement.

The inauguration of the tabernacle saw it covered in a supernatural cloud. Exodus 40:34-35 says, "Then the cloud covered the tent of meeting, and the glory of the LORD filled the tabernacle. Moses could not enter the tent of meeting because the cloud had settled on it, and the glory of the LORD filled the tabernacle." Something similar happened when the temple replaced the tabernacle and the priests were forced to evacuate (1 Kings 8:10-11). Now on the mount of transfiguration the cloud again descends as God meets humanity in the person of Christ.

No wonder the disciples are afraid as the cloud envelops them. This is uncharted territory. Only Moses and the high priests have been here before. And their experience was surrounded by caveats and warnings. Can human beings really enter the cloud of God's glory? Can we meet God and live?

The answer is: yes! What makes this difference is Jesus. "For in Christ all the fullness of the Deity lives in bodily form" (Colossians 2:9). Through the cross, God "has reconciled you by Christ's physical body through death to present you holy in his sight, without blemish and free from accusation" (1:22). Jesus has defused the threat of God's holiness—not by making God any less holy but by making us "holy in his sight".

MEDITATION

Arise, my soul, arise,
Shake off your guilty fears:
The perfect Sacrifice
On my behalf appears.
Before the throne my Surety stands,
My name is written on his hands.

He ever lives above,
For me to intercede;
His all-redeeming love,
His precious blood to plead.
His blood atoned for ev'ry race,
And sprinkles now the throne of grace.

My God is reconciled;
His pardoning voice I hear.
He owns me for his child,
I can no longer fear.
With confidence I now draw nigh,
And "Father, Abba, Father!" cry.

(Charles Wesley)

TUESDAY

Peter and his companions were very sleepy, but
when they became fully awake, they saw his glory.

LUKE 9:32

In Luke's account of the transfiguration, Peter, James, and John are singled out to pray with Jesus and we're also told they are sleepy. Does that remind you of anything? Luke is clearly linking the transfiguration to the Garden of Gethsemane. So let's move on to another mountain. For in Luke's Gospel, the mount of transfiguration also leads us to the Mount of Olives, the location of the Garden of Gethsemane.

Jesus went out as usual to the Mount of Olives, and
his disciples followed him. On reaching the place,
he said to them, "Pray that you will not fall into
temptation." He withdrew about a stone's throw
beyond them, knelt down and prayed, "Father, if
you are willing, take this cup from me; yet not my
will, but yours be done." An angel from heaven
appeared to him and strengthened him. And being
in anguish, he prayed more earnestly, and his sweat
was like drops of blood falling to the ground.

When he rose from prayer and went back to the disciples, he found them asleep, exhausted from sorrow. "Why are you sleeping?" he asked them. "Get up and pray so that you will not fall into temptation." (Luke 22:39-46)

The first thing we notice is that Luke's account doesn't focus on Peter, James and John—that comes from Matthew and Mark's accounts. And his account doesn't actually take place in the Garden of Gethsemane—again that comes from Matthew and Mark. Luke locates it more generally on the Mount of Olives. What this does is heighten the link to the transfiguration. Luke is giving us two mountain-top experiences: one of glory and one of pain.

On the mount of transfiguration, the divinity of Christ "shines" through. On the Mount of Olives, his humanity, as it were, "shines" through. At the transfiguration, "the appearance of his face changed" as the glory of his divinity was displayed on his face. On the Mount of Olives, the appearance of his face also changed, but this time it is because Jesus sweats drops of blood (Luke 22:44). The flesh-and-blood humanity of Christ is literally displayed on his face.

The disciples need to see his divinity (as they do on the mount of transfiguration) so that they understand his death as part of God's plan. God has entered history in the person of Jesus. As a human being Jesus shares our pain and confusion. As God he brings his life and light. He shines into our darkness with the light of his love. "Peter, James and John are allowed to see Christ's glory so that when they witness his anguish and death they may know that these terrible moments are freely embraced by the God-made-human who is Jesus, and held within the infinite depth of life."[26]

"During the days of Jesus' life on earth," says Hebrews 5:7, Jesus "offered up prayers and petitions with fervent cries and tears". It's an allusion to Gethsemane. Jesus experienced our humanity to the full. All the weight of our brokenness and guilt was being lowered onto his shoulders, and in Gethsemane it threatened to over-whelm him. He knows what it's like to be you in all your weakness. As a result, "he is able to deal gently with those who are ignorant and are going astray, since he himself is subject to weakness" (5:2).

Today Jesus deals gently with your brokenness and guilt. So don't hesitate to bring that brokenness and guilt in prayer to a God who is gloriously radiant yet personally understands your hurt and frailty.

MEDITATION

A Man there is, a real Man,
With wounds still gaping wide,
From which rich streams of blood once ran,
In hands, and feet, and side.
'Tis no wild fancy of our brains,
No metaphor we speak;
The same dear Man in heaven now reigns
That suffered for our sake.
That human heart he still retains,
Though throned in highest bliss;
And feels each tempted member's pains;
For our affliction's his.
Come, then, repenting sinner, come.
Approach with humble faith.
Owe what thou wilt, the total sum
Is cancelled by his death.

(Joseph Hart)

WEDNESDAY

*Since, then, you have been raised with
Christ, set your hearts on things above.*

COLOSSIANS 3:1

A number of the Greek church fathers saw the transfiguration as a pattern for contemplative prayer. It's certainly striking that Luke adds two references to prayer in his account of the transfiguration. Jesus takes the disciples up the mountain "to pray" and Jesus is transfigured "as he was praying" (Luke 9:28, 29). The 19th-century Scottish preacher Robert Murray McCheyne comments, "Christ loved to pray alone … Christ loved secret prayer".[27]

To pray is to meet with God. And where is the place where we can meet God? Once it was Mount Sinai, but not anymore. Once it was the tabernacle and then the Jerusalem Temple, but not anymore. Now, that meeting place is Jesus himself. If we want to meet God, then the place to go is Jesus!

The disciples climbed up the mount of transfiguration to encounter God—just as Moses had done at Mount Sinai. In a similar way, we ascend by faith into the presence of God through the mediation of Christ. "Since, then, you have been raised with Christ, set your hearts on things above, where Christ is, seated at the right hand of God" (Colossians 3:1). In the presence of God we find ourselves surrounded by his fatherly love and protected by his heavenly power.

- *An important aspect of prayer is to enjoy being in God's presence as we experience that through the Holy Spirit. So, like the disciples on the mount of transfiguration, let us ascend by faith to meet God in Christ.*

Prayer includes contemplating the glory of God. But we no longer have to hide in a rock to see God's glory as Moses did (Exodus 33:21-23). Now we see "God's glory displayed in the face of Christ" (2 Corinthians 4:6). The story of the transfiguration is an invitation to enjoy the radiant beauty of Christ.

- *An important aspect of prayer is to contemplate the glory of Christ in the story of the gospel. So, like the disciples on the mount of transfiguration, let us gaze by faith on God in Christ.*

Luke also links the transfiguration to Christ's agonised prayer in Gethsemane with his description of Peter, James and John being sleepy (Luke 9:32). Jesus both begins and ends his time of prayer on the Mount of Olives by exhorting the disciples to prayer: "Why are you sleeping? ... Get up and pray so that you will not fall into temptation" (Luke 22:40, 46).

Jesus presents falling into temptation and praying to God as alternatives. That's because we can't stand in our own strength. We need to seek God for his divine enabling. Moreover, enjoying God's presence and beholding Christ's glory in prayer are powerful antidotes to the attractions of sin.

- *An important aspect of prayer is to find the strength to resist temptation. So, like the disciples were called to do on the Mount of Olives, how can you watch and pray today?*

MEDITATION

*"Come, let us ascend the spiritual mountain
of contemplation,
and let us gaze at the view from there,
attentively and free from material considerations."*

*(The 14th-century theologian
Gregory the Sinaite)*[28]

THURSDAY

But he was pierced for our transgressions,
he was crushed for our iniquities.

ISAIAH 53:5

We've seen how Luke has embedded allusions in his account of the transfiguration: from the mount of transfiguration to Mount Sinai and then to the Mount of Olives. Finally, Luke leads us to the hill of Calvary.

Luke includes the phrase "whom I have chosen" in his account of the words of the voice from heaven (Luke 9:35). Matthew and Mark leave these words out. It's an allusion to Isaiah 42:1 where God says, "Here is my servant, whom I uphold, my chosen one in whom I delight".

God is introducing his servant—the one who will "open eyes that are blind" and "free captives from prison" (42:7). This is the first of four songs in the book of Isaiah that speak of the servant of the Lord. They culminate in Isaiah 53 where the servant accomplishes salvation by suffering in the place of God's people (53:4-6). The servant is the *suffering* servant.

Here, in the midst of his transfigured glory, Luke is portraying Jesus as that suffering servant.

Luke says that at the transfiguration "the appearance of his face changed" (Luke 9:29). Matthew is more explicit about what this involved: "His face shone like the sun" (Matthew 17:2). But Luke is more ambiguous with his description: he simply says that the appearance of Jesus changed. I think this is because, even as Jesus is revealed in glory, Luke knows that soon "his appearance" will be "disfigured beyond that of any human being"—another quote from one of Isaiah's Servant Songs (Isaiah 52:14). At the transfiguration, Christ is human but also more than human as his divinity is revealed. Soon, Christ will be human but also appear less than human as his humanity is disfigured. Isaiah goes on:

> *He had no beauty or majesty to attract us to him,*
> *nothing in his appearance that we should*
> *desire him.*
> *He was despised and rejected by mankind,*
> *a man of suffering, and familiar with pain.*
> *Isaiah 53:2-3*

A disfigured saviour with no desirable features is not an attractive saviour. So humanity rejects him. "We considered him punished by God," Isaiah continues (53:4).

But faith enables us to look beyond the disfigurement and see glory, the glory of love. "He was pierced for our transgressions," says Isaiah, "he was crushed for our iniquities" (v 5). In his love Jesus bore the penalty of our sin in our place. The result is his disfigurement, and we despise him for it. And yet it is for us! "By his wounds we are healed" (v 5).

Humanity despises the crucified Christ. But this is God the Father's verdict: he is "my chosen one in whom I delight". Will you join the Father in delighting in Jesus and his cross today?

MEDITATION

"Here, in the midst of his transfiguration,
[Moses and Elijah] speak of his passion ...
A strange opportunity, in his highest exaltation,
to speak of his sufferings ...
when his head shone with glory,
to tell him how it must bleed with thorns;
when his face shone like the sun,
to tell him it must be blubbered and spat upon;
when his garments glistered with
celestial brightness,
to tell him they must be stripped and divided ...
and whilst he was Transfigured on the Mount,
to tell him how he must be Disfigured
on the Cross!

(The 17th-century bishop Joseph Hall)[29]

FRIDAY

*Two men, Moses and Elijah, appeared in
glorious splendour, talking with Jesus.*

LUKE 9:30

I once went with a friend to watch England play India at cricket. We arrived early and saw Joe Root—one of my cricketing heroes—warming up on the out-field. "Go and talk to him," my friend urged. I declined. What was I going to say? "Hello, you're Joe Root"?

If you were to meet your hero, what would you say?

On the mount of transfiguration, Moses and Elijah get to meet not just their hero but their Lord and God. What do they say?

Luke tells us. "Two men, Moses and Elijah," he writes, "appeared in glorious splendour, talking with Jesus". Then Luke adds, "They spoke about his departure" (Luke 9:30-31). It's literally "his exodus". It's an allusion to the story of the exodus—when God rescued his people from slavery in Egypt. But it's also another reference to Isaiah (as we saw in the previous chapter), one of the key themes in Isaiah's prophecy is the promise of a *new* exodus.

The exodus was the defining story for Israel. God had come down, seen the misery of his people, and rescued them through ten mighty plagues. The final plague had brought death on every firstborn child in Egypt, but the Israelites had escaped by offering a lamb. Through this "Passover" lamb, God's judgment had "passed over" his people. The Israelites had then passed through the Red Sea to a new life with God. At Mount Sinai, they entered into a covenant with God through which he became their God and they became his people. So the exodus defined who God was: he was their covenant Lord who had redeemed them. And it defined who they were: they were the people formed by God's redemption.

Isaiah saw in that story the framework for a new and bigger work of God—not simply an exodus from human tyranny but a *new exodus* from sin and death. This promise of a new exodus shaped the way the apostles understood the significance of the death and resurrection of Christ. Let's take just one example:

> *This is what the* LORD *says—*
> *he who made a way through the sea,*
> *a path through the mighty waters,*
> *who drew out the chariots and horses,*
> *the army and reinforcements together,*
> *and they lay there, never to rise again,*
> *extinguished, snuffed out like a wick:*
> *"Forget the former things;*
> *do not dwell on the past.*
> *See, I am doing a new thing!*
> *Now it springs up; do you not perceive it?*
> *I am making a way in the wilderness*

and streams in the wasteland.
The wild animals honour me,
  the jackals and the owls,
because I provide water in the wilderness
  and streams in the wasteland,
to give drink to my people, my chosen,
the people I formed for myself
  that they may proclaim my praise.

(Isaiah 43:16-21)

Isaiah reminds us that the Lord led his people through the Red Sea as they escaped from Pharaoh and then destroyed the Egyptian army under the waves (Exodus 14). But now God says, in effect, *Stop looking back to the exodus from Egypt because I'm going to do something new, something bigger, something better.* It's this new exodus that Jesus, Moses and Elijah discuss on the mount of transfiguration. It's bigger because it will encompass all nations, and it's better because it liberates us from sin and judgment.

At the first exodus, God provided streams in the desert to quench the physical thirst of his people (Exodus 15, 17). And Isaiah says that "water in the wilderness and streams in the wasteland" (Isaiah 43:20) will be a feature of the new exodus. So it is that, in fulfilment of that promise, Jesus offers to quench our spiritual thirst: "Whoever believes in me, as Scripture has said, rivers of living water will flow from within them" (John 7:38; see also 4:13-14).

The result is that we are a people formed for Jesus that we might proclaim his praise (Isaiah 43:21). If you're a Christian, Christ has liberated you from sin, rescued you from death, brought you into his people, and made spiritual life bubble up within you through his Spirit. How are you going to praise him today?

MEDITATION

*"Christ, our Passover lamb, has been sacrificed.
Therefore let us keep the Festival,
not with the old bread leavened with malice
and wickedness,
but with the unleavened bread of sincerity
and truth."*

(1 Corinthians 5:7-8)

SATURDAY

Suddenly, when they looked around, they no longer saw anyone with them except Jesus.

MARK 9:8

The Australian scholar Peter Bolt compares the transfiguration story to "translation stories". Translation stories are stories that involve people being taken up to heaven. They exist in mythologies around the world. But they're also present in the Bible story. For example, Elijah was taken up to heaven in a whirlwind (2 Kings 2:11-12). An extensive search was made for his body, but it couldn't be found (2:15-18).

Bolt also compares the transfiguration to "apotheosis stories"—a Greek idea that virtuous people might escape this body and unite with the deity. It has some biblical precedent in the story of Enoch, though both Enoch's soul *and body* are taken up to heaven (Genesis 5:22-24).

The Romans created their own version of these stories when they started deifying the emperors. Rather than simply dying, emperors were said to have become gods. They claimed they were transported or translated from human existence to divine existence.

At first sight, the transfiguration looks like one of these translation or apotheosis stories. Jesus is glorified as heaven touches earth and eternity touches time. But there are a couple of crucial differences. The obvious one is that Jesus is not transformed into something new. He does not transform into God once he's on the mountain. Instead, what has always been in himself becomes apparent to those around him. The medieval theologian Thomas Aquinas says, "[Jesus] is transfigured not by receiving what he was not, but manifesting to his disciples what he was".[30]

But there is another significant difference. Mark says, "Suddenly, when they looked around, they no longer saw anyone with them except Jesus" (Mark 9:8). When all the fireworks have subsided, there's only one person left, and it's the person who might have been expected to be taken away. We might have expected the story to end with everyone watching Jesus disappear into the skies (as would happen at his ascension). But instead, everyone else leaves and only Jesus remains with the disciples.

If it's virtuous people—like Enoch and Elijah—who by-pass death and go straight to heaven, then surely Jesus is the top contender. He alone of all humanity did not deserve to die. But Jesus chose to remain on earth. He chose to set out from the mount of transfiguration to the hill of Calvary, to walk to his death. Why? Why embrace a fate he did not deserve and could have escaped? Because before time began, he and the Father had planned and agreed together to create and redeem a people with whom they would share their love.

Peter Bolt comments:

> *[Jesus] rejected the opportunity to avoid death*
> *through translation or apotheosis and embraced*
> *his future suffering for the sake of the divine plan.*
> *Thus, in the transfiguration, Jesus continued in his*
> *resolve to walk the path of the suffering servant.*
> *There would have been no resurrection and no glo-*
> *rious kingdom of God without his prior suffering.*
> *From that point onwards, the narrative pressed*
> *relentlessly forward to his inevitable death.*[31]

Shortly after the transfiguration, Luke writes, "As the time approached for him to be taken up to heaven, Jesus resolutely set out for Jerusalem" (Luke 9:51). Jesus is heading for heaven, but his route will take him through Jerusalem and via the cross.

The glory of Jesus is not simply the light-show on the mount of transfiguration. His ultimate glory is his determination to offer himself for his people. It is the glory of his love. And so the mount of transfiguration leads to the hill of Calvary. His reward is not simply to be glorified but to lead his people home to glory. He is not only victorious over sin and death; he shares that victory with us.

MEDITATION

Jesus replied:
"Now my soul is troubled, and what shall I say?
'Father, save me from this hour'?
No, it was for this very reason I came to this hour.
Father, glorify your name!"

Then a voice came from heaven,
"I have glorified it, and will glorify it again" …

Jesus said,
"This voice was for your benefit, not mine …
And I, when I am lifted up from the earth,
will draw all people to myself."
He said this to show the kind of death he was going to die.

(John 12:27-33)

THE
RADIANT
VICTORY
OF JESUS

THE FIFTH WEEK OF LENT

SUNDAY

This week we come back to Mark's account. This time round we're going to focus on what happens just before and just after the transfiguration. Let's start with what comes before:

> *And he said to them, "Truly I tell you, some who are standing here will not taste death before they see that the kingdom of God has come with power." After six days Jesus took Peter, James and John with him and led them up a high mountain.*   *(Mark 9:1-2)*

Mark does not generally use specific time references. So it's significant that he identifies that six days passed between the statement of verse 1 and the events of verse 2. He clearly intends to tie them together.

Take time to read these verses through a couple of times, preferably aloud.

- *Of those who heard this statement from Jesus, who did see the kingdom of God come with power and how?*

MONDAY

*"Some who are standing here will not
taste death before they see that the kingdom
of God has come with power."*

MARK 9:1

Let's dive straight into the glaring question raised by the words of Mark 9:1: what is Jesus talking about when he speaks of the kingdom coming in power? It seems that he might be describing his return at the end of time (especially since he's just talked about that in Mark 8:38). Yet he also says that some of his hearers will see this in their lifetime.

The early chapters of Mark portray Jesus exercising God's authority. He calls followers, commands demons, speaks with authority, heals the sick and forgives sin (Mark 1:16 – 2:12). All the evidence points to Jesus being God's King, sent by him. But Jesus is also rejected and opposed (2:1 – 3:6). That wasn't part of anyone's expectation of God's King. The Jews expected God's kingdom to sweep away all before it and bring judgment on God's enemies.

So, is Jesus God's King and is this God's kingdom? Jesus addresses these questions in the parables of Mark 4. He says that the Jewish expectations were spot on: God's

King will come in power. One day his kingdom will extend throughout the world—but not yet. First it comes secretly in grace. The kingdom grows through the preaching of the word (like the sowing of seed) and it brings the offer of forgiveness. As we've seen already, we're all enemies of God. If the kingdom were to come in power, then we would all be defeated. So, first Christ comes, not to dispense judgment, but to bear judgment. When judgment falls at the first coming of Jesus, it falls at the cross on the King himself in the place of his people.

This coming in grace doesn't cancel or replace the future coming in power. That day is still coming, and when it does come, God's kingdom will be the only show in town. But that moment has several previews.

Think of a big movie. Before its release, the movie company issues trailers to give a taste of what's to come. The return of Christ in glory is the big movie. Its release date is unknown. But God has given us a number of trailers—both to confirm it's on its way and to provide a preview of what it will be like:

1. *It was previewed in the fall of Jerusalem when the temple and the system it represented were brought to an end (Mark 13).*

2. *It was previewed at the resurrection and ascension of Jesus. Jesus has been acclaimed by heaven as God's King. He has received all authority, even though that authority is not yet exercised in judgment (Matthew 28:18-19).*

3. *It was previewed six days after Jesus speaks these*
   words in Mark 9:1, at the transfiguration when the
   power of Christ was made manifest in his physical
   appearance.

So, the ultimate fulfilment of Christ's words are his
return, when humanity will be judged and he will be
glorified. Yet Jesus can still say some of his hearers "will
not taste death" before they see this because they will be
eye-witnesses of its anticipations in the transfiguration,
resurrection, ascension, and the fall of Jerusalem. The
theologian Donald Macleod concludes, "[The transfiguration is] a pre-vision ... of the entire exaltation of Jesus,
including resurrection, ascension and heavenly session;
and including also the Parousia [the coming at the end
of time]".[32]

When Christ returns, he will not receive glory for
the first time; instead, the glory he already has will be
revealed to the world. That's why the New Testament
describes his return as his "appearance" or "manifesta-
tion". This is our hope and consolation in troubled
times: "When Christ, who is your life, appears, then
you also will appear with him in glory" (Colossians 3:4).
Hold on today to that preview of his glory—knowing
that the main event is coming soon.

MEDITATION

Jesus, my Lord, my life, my light,
Oh come with blissful ray.
Break radiant through the shades of night
And chase my fears away.
Then shall my soul with rapture trace,
The wonders of your love.
But the full glories of your face
Are only known above.

(From "O lovely source of true delight" by Anne Steele)

TUESDAY

They will say, "Where is this 'coming' he promised?
Ever since our ancestors died, everything goes
on as it has since the beginning of creation."

2 PETER 3:4

Here's another puzzle that the transfiguration throws in our direction: did it take place six days or eight days after the words of Mark 9:1? We've seen how significant it is that Mark begins his account with "after six days" (v 2). It links the transfiguration to the promise of Christ's return and perhaps also suggests that Jesus is the beginning of a new humanity (revealed on the sixth day just as Adam was created on the sixth day). So why does Luke say the transfiguration took place "about eight days after Jesus said this" (Luke 9:28)?

At one level it's a historical question. How many days later was it? Is Mark correct or Luke? The answer is to recognise how ancient people spoke of the passing of days. For example, the Bible often speaks of Jesus being raised on the third day. But in fact, today we would describe Sunday as two days after Friday. How you count an interval of time depends on whether you choose to include the days of the first and second events. Luke's eight days are Mark's six intervening days, plus the day on which Jesus was speaking, plus the day on which Jesus was transfigured. Don Carson says that Luke's phrasing "is based on a Greek way of speaking and means 'about a week later'".[33] So Mark and Luke are both right; they're just using slightly different ways of counting.

But Luke's inclusion of eight days also raises a *theological* question: what does Luke's choice to spotlight eight days reveal about his message? I think the answer is that eight is seven plus one. I know you knew that already! Here's the point. The world was made in six days. On the seventh day God rested. That means the eighth day is when the process begins again. For Luke this doesn't mean week two in the history of the world. For Luke this means a new creation in which the world is made new. God made the world in six days and rested on the seventh. Now on the eighth day he is beginning to *remake* the world.

If that's correct, then the transfiguration is not just an anticipation of the future of Christ; it's also an anticipation of Christ's new humanity and his new world. Christians are heading for glory and for a brief moment in history, on the mount of transfiguration, we were given a glimpse of that coming glory.

The transfiguration anticipates the triumph of God's kingdom and God's King. This may be one reason why Peter spotlights the transfiguration in 2 Peter 1. The return of Christ is what was being disputed among Peter's readers. Scoffers will come, warns Peter, saying, "Where is this 'coming' he promised?" (3:4). As we've seen, Peter refers to the story of the transfiguration in

2 Peter 1:16-18 to show that the apostles were eyewitnesses of what had taken place *in the past* during the first coming of Jesus. But one reason Peter chose to focus specifically on the transfiguration is that this story shows the apostles were also witnesses of what will be *in the future*. The future promises of the Bible are confirmed by the foretaste they received at the transfiguration. We can be sure Christ will return in glory because humanity has already glimpsed his glory on the mountain.

Look around the world today and you will see what Peter's readers saw: everything goes on as it always has. It's easy for the return of Christ to feel like a distant reality that makes little difference to my Tuesday morning. But when we look at the transfiguration, we see heaven pushing into earthly realities—like a nail gently pushing into a balloon. One day heaven will burst through and the new age will dawn.

MEDITATION

"Peter and the sons of thunder saw
His beauty on the mountain,
outshining the brightness of the sun,
and they were deemed worthy to receive
the anticipation of His glorious Coming with their eyes."

(The 4th-century theologian St Basil the Great)[34]

WEDNESDAY

*Now I know in part; then I shall know
fully, even as I am fully known.*

1 CORINTHIANS 13:12

"I'm so glad to see you," we sometimes say. Perhaps we're in need and someone has come to our aid. Perhaps we've been separated from a loved one and now we're reunited. Seeing can fill us with gladness.

Jesus promised that his hearers would "see" the kingdom of God in Mark 9:1. That sight is anticipated in the transfiguration. But how? Let me suggest a couple of ways that the transfiguration anticipates God's coming new world.

First, at the transfiguration Jesus remained Jesus even though he was transformed. Jesus didn't become someone else. The disciples could recognise the radiant figure before them. He was the same person. And yet, in another sense, he wasn't the same at all: he was gloriously transfigured and transformed.

This pattern of the-same-but-not-the-same will be what happens to all creation when Christ returns. The new creation is not "new" in the sense of completely replacing our broken world. It will be our world, but our world wonderfully renewed and transformed. It's not so much "brand new" as "made new" or "renewed". It will be our world *minus* sin, suffering and brokenness and it will be our world *plus* holiness, wholeness and glory.

In my part of the world, we get a little picture of this with every fall of snow. I love walking out into the countryside around my home after the snow has fallen (especially if I'm the first person to walk through it). It's a landscape I know well and even covered in snow, it's still familiar. I don't get lost! I can still trace the contours of the hills, see the trees and hedges, search out the footpaths. It's the same place. And yet it's not the same. It's as if it's been made new. All the mess and mud have been covered over in the radiant covering of snow. Just for a moment, in those first few hours, it feels as if everything becomes "dazzling white" (Mark 9:3). It's only an illustration, but it gives a sense of what it might feel like to stand in the new creation.

The transfiguration anticipates God's new world in a second way. At the transfiguration the focus was all on Jesus, and in the human body of Jesus the disciples saw something of the glory of God. But it will be no different in the new creation. For all the radiance of a world-made-new, the focus will be on Jesus. He will out-dazzle the dazzle of everything else. And in Jesus we will see God.

Throughout the centuries theologians have said the story of redemption will culminate in what they have called "the beatific vision": we will see God. "For now we see only a reflection as in a mirror;" says Paul in 1 Corinthians 13:12, "then we shall see face to face".

But how will finite human beings see the infinite God? How will eyes see the God who is invisible? Part of the answer is that we will see God in Christ. In seeing Christ's glorified human body, we will see the glory of his whole person. But the Person of Christ cannot be separated from the Persons of the Father and the Spirit since they share one divine essence. Our physical eyes (albeit eyes which will then be part of glorified bodies) will see the physical body of Christ, but as we look at him, we will see the glory of God. This is what Peter, James and John saw on the mount of transfiguration, albeit in a limited form adapted to their capacities at the time. "Blessed are the pure in heart," promises Jesus, "for they will see God" (Matthew 5:8).

The word "beatific" doesn't mean "beautiful"—though it will be a beautiful sight. It means "blessed" or "bless-ing-bringing". The 18th-century American theologian Jonathan Edwards called it the "happifying" vision.[35] This vision of God in Christ will make us happier than ever, for ever.

MEDITATION

"Dear friends, now we are children of God,
and what we will be has not yet been made known.
But we know that when Christ appears,
we shall be like him,
for we shall see him as he is.
All who have this hope in him purify themselves,
just as he is pure." (1 John 3:2-3)

THURSDAY

*Jesus gave them orders not to tell anyone
what they had seen until the Son of
Man had risen from the dead.*

MARK 9:9

The transfiguration is a trailer for the coming of the kingdom of God in glory. But we mustn't get ahead of ourselves. In the meantime, we still live in the confusion of this present age. Mark addresses this in the stories that follow his account of the transfiguration.

As they were coming down the mountain, Jesus gave them orders not to tell anyone what they had seen until the Son of Man had risen from the dead. They kept the matter to themselves, discussing what "rising from the dead" meant.

And they asked him, "Why do the teachers of the law say that Elijah must come first?"

Jesus replied, "To be sure, Elijah does come first, and restores all things. Why then is it written that the Son of Man must suffer much and be rejected? But I tell you, Elijah has come, and they have done to him everything they wished, just as it is written about him." (Mark 9:9-13)

Verses 9-10 are the key example of a phenomenon that scholars have called "the messianic secret". Jesus is committed to preaching. On at least one occasion he spurns the opportunity to perform miracles so he can get on with the task of preaching—"that is why I have come," he explains (1:35-39). And yet, at key moments in Mark's Gospel, Jesus stops people preaching. He warns people not to tell anyone what he has done for them. When he heals a man with leprosy, for example, Jesus says, "See that you don't tell this to anyone" (1:40-45). Or when Peter confesses Jesus to be the Messiah, Jesus responds by warning the disciples "not to tell anyone about him" (8:29-30). And again, as they come down from the mountain, Jesus tells Peter, James and John "not to tell anyone" what they have just witnessed (9:9). He seems to want to keep his messianic identity a secret.

Why does Jesus forbid people from revealing his identity? The answer is that Jesus doesn't want to be proclaimed as the Messiah until people realise he's the *suffering* Messiah. To proclaim him as the Messiah is misleading if people have a wrong conception of what that means.

But, notice there's a time limit on this prohibition! It has what today we would call "a sunset clause". A law with a sunset clause has its own end written into the wording. During the COVID pandemic, for example, some governments introduced restrictions that would automatically cease after a built-in period of time. Once Jesus has died and risen, then the power revealed in his miracles and the glory revealed in his transfiguration can be proclaimed—once we also know that he's the suffering Messiah who has died in our place.

So there are no prohibitions on preaching Jesus today. Quite the opposite. Jesus left us with a commission to call the nations to follow him. But the rationale for his no-preaching sunset clause remains: we cannot preach Jesus without preaching the cross. Jesus is not simply a model for us to follow; he's the Saviour who died to pay the price of our sin. He's not just a healer who meets our felt needs; he's the re-creator who transforms us from the inside out. He's not just a teacher with wisdom for a happy life; he's the Lord who calls us to deny ourselves, take up our cross and follow him. Who will you tell of his suffering and glory today?

MEDITATION

We sing the praise of him who died,
Of him who died upon the cross:
The sinner's hope, let men deride,
For this we count the world but loss.

Inscribed upon the cross we see
In shining letters, "God is love".
He bears our sins upon the tree;
He brings us mercy from above.

The cross! It takes our guilt away.
It holds the fainting spirit up.
It cheers with hope the gloomy day,
And sweetens every bitter cup.

It makes the coward spirit brave,
And nerves the feeble arm for fight.
It takes its terror from the grave,
And gilds the bed of death with light:

The balm of life, the cure of woe,
The measure and the pledge of love,
The sinner's refuge here below,
The angels' theme in heaven above.

(Thomas Kelly)

FRIDAY

*"Why do the teachers of the law say
that Elijah must come first?"*

MARK 9:11

I guess that Peter, James and John were pretty excited as they walked down the mountain. They had positive proof that Jesus was the Messiah. But he had now told them not to tell anyone, which might have put a bit of a dampener on things. How were they going to keep quiet about the glory they had just witnessed? Surely the victory of God was just a few days away, a few weeks at most?

But there was a problem. The timeline didn't quite stack up as they expected. So, as they come down the mountain, the disciples ask Jesus a question, "Why do the teachers of the law say that Elijah must come first?" (Mark 9:11). They've just seen something that looks pretty much like the coming of God's kingdom. But people said Elijah would come first as a forerunner of God's Messiah. So how can they have witnessed God's kingdom if Elijah hasn't yet returned?

Jesus replies, "To be sure, Elijah does come first, and restores all things. Why then is it written that the Son of Man must suffer much and be rejected? But I tell you,

Elijah has come, and they have done to him everything they wished, just as it is written about him" (v 12-13). In effect Jesus is saying that Elijah has returned in the form of John the Baptist (Mark 9:12). Indeed, Mark's presentation of John the Baptist in Mark 1:2-8 is clearly intended to echo descriptions of Elijah. Both of them can be recognised because each has "a garment of hair" and "a leather belt round his waist" (2 Kings 1:8; Mark 1:6). Matthew makes this connection to John the Baptist explicit by adding, "Then the disciples understood that he was talking to them about John the Baptist" (Matthew 17:13). So we're not waiting for something to happen before God's King comes. The forerunner has already done his job. The time is now. The time has come. The Messiah is here—talking with the disciples as they walk down the mountain.

But what Jesus really wants the disciples to focus on is this: the Messiah must suffer. "Why then is it written," he adds, "that the Son of Man must suffer much and be rejected? But I tell you, Elijah has come, and they have done to him everything they wished, just as it is written about him" (Mark 9:12-13). Elijah had returned in the person of John the Baptist and what had happened to him? Herod had killed him (6:14-29). And the fate of the forerunner is a pointer to the fate of the King. What's coming next in the timeline is not victory, but the weakness, folly and shame of the cross.

Peter, James and John see a great vision of the glory of Jesus. Peter wants to stay gazing at it for ever (9:5-6). But God will ultimately be revealed on the cross. It's in the weakness of the cross that we see the power of God. It's in the folly of the cross that we see the wisdom of God. It's in the shame of the cross that we see the glory of God.

And that's exactly what happens. The centurion confesses that Jesus is "the Son of God" as he "stood there in front of Jesus" hanging on the cross and "saw how he died" (Mark 15:39). Peter wants to see the glory of Jesus on the mountain for ever, but it cannot be. The other disciples don't see the transfiguration at all. And neither do Mark's readers and neither do we. But we *can* see God revealed in the message of the cross.

Today we can't give people visions of glory. But we can reveal God to them as we proclaim the message of the cross.

MEDITATION

"For the message of the cross is foolishness to
those who are perishing, but to us who are
being saved it is the power of God ...
Jews demand signs and Greeks look for wisdom,
but we preach Christ crucified:
a stumbling-block to Jews and foolishness to
Gentiles, but to those whom God has called,
both Jews and Greeks,
Christ the power of God and the wisdom of God.
For the foolishness of God is wiser than human wisdom,
and the weakness of God is stronger than human strength."

(1 Corinthians 1:18, 22-25)

SATURDAY

Peter, James and John have just had an amazing experience of God. Life is never going to be the same again. Perhaps it felt like anything was possible. But they arrived at the bottom of the mountain with a bit of a bump. They walk straight into a messy situation. The challenges of life on earth are alive and kicking.

When they came to the other disciples, they saw a large crowd around them and the teachers of the law arguing with them. As soon as all the people saw Jesus, they were overwhelmed with wonder and ran to greet him.

"What are you arguing with them about?" he asked.

A man in the crowd answered, "Teacher, I brought you my son, who is possessed by a spirit that has robbed him of speech. Whenever it seizes him, it throws him to the ground. He foams at the mouth, gnashes his teeth and becomes rigid.

I asked your disciples to drive out the spirit, but they could not."

"You unbelieving generation," Jesus replied, "how long shall I stay with you? How long shall I put up with you? Bring the boy to me."

So they brought him. When the spirit saw Jesus, it immediately threw the boy into a convulsion. He fell to the ground and rolled around, foaming at the mouth.

Jesus asked the boy's father, "How long has he been like this?"

"From childhood," he answered. "It has often thrown him into fire or water to kill him. But if you can do anything, take pity on us and help us."

"'If you can'?" said Jesus. "Everything is possible for one who believes."

Immediately the boy's father exclaimed, "I do believe; help me overcome my unbelief!"

When Jesus saw that a crowd was running to the scene, he rebuked the impure spirit. "You deaf and mute spirit," he said, "I command you, come out of him and never enter him again."

The spirit shrieked, convulsed him violently and came out. The boy looked so much like a corpse that many said, "He's dead." But Jesus took him by the hand and lifted him to his feet, and he stood up.

After Jesus had gone indoors, his disciples asked him privately, "Why couldn't we drive it out?"

He replied, "This kind can come out only by prayer."   *(Mark 9:14-29)*

How will the disciples get on when Jesus is not around? And for that matter, how can you and I? In the case of the disciples, the answer would appear to be: not very well. The scene depicted in Mark 9:14-29 echoes Exodus 32 where Moses comes down from Sinai having seen the glory of God to find the unfaithful Israelites worshipping the golden calf. The problem is set out by Jesus in Mark 9:19: "You unbelieving generation". "Why couldn't we drive it out?" the disciples ask in Matthew 17:19. Jesus answers, "Because you have so little faith" (v 20).

The important thing is not whether we see Jesus or indeed a miraculous sign, but instead to believe the message of the cross. We're to believe the words of Jesus and not be ashamed of them (Mark 8:38). We're to trust Jesus even though we can't physically see him.

We have a lovely model for this in Mark 9:24: "Immediately the boy's father exclaimed, 'I do believe; help me overcome my unbelief!'" Here we see trust mingled with humility and expressed in prayer. When we can't see God at work, Mark is telling us, we need to ask God to strengthen our faith. "After Jesus had gone indoors, his disciples asked him privately, 'Why couldn't we drive it out?' He replied, 'This kind can come out only by prayer'" (Mark 9:28-29). Even when we cannot see

Jesus, we can know his presence through prayer. We're not out of touch. We're not cut off.

Jesus has ascended into heaven, but God is still revealed in the message of the cross. And consider what happens when that message is proclaimed:

- *The deaf will hear. "'You deaf and mute spirit,' he said, 'I command you, come out of him and never enter him again'" (v 25). The remarkable thing is that Jesus speaks to a deaf man! What an encouragement to us when people seem deaf to the message of the gospel.*

- *Those in Satan's power will be released. "The spirit shrieked, convulsed him violently and came out" (v 26). Perhaps you can't imagine some people ever becoming Christians. Well, this boy was an unlikely convert, but a word from Jesus set him free.*

- *The dead will find life. "The boy looked so much like a corpse that many said, 'He's dead.' But Jesus took him by the hand and lifted him to his feet, and he stood up" (v 27). It's a picture of the life-changing power of the Holy Spirit to grant spiritual life to dead souls at the behest of Jesus.*

MEDITATION

'Tis good, Lord, to be here!
Your glory fills the night;
Your face and garments, like the sun,
Shine with unborrowed light.
'Tis good, Lord, to be here!
Yet we may not remain;
But since you bid us leave the mount,
Come with us to the plain.

(Joseph A. Robinson)

RADIANT AND TRANS-FORMED

HOLY WEEK & EASTER SUNDAY

SUNDAY

There's one more account of the transfiguration that we've not yet looked at: Matthew's account.

After six days Jesus took with him Peter, James and John the brother of James, and led them up a high mountain by themselves. There he was transfigured before them. His face shone like the sun, and his clothes became as white as the light. Just then there appeared before them Moses and Elijah, talking with Jesus.

Peter said to Jesus, "Lord, it is good for us to be here. If you wish, I will put up three shelters—one for you, one for Moses and one for Elijah."

While he was still speaking, a bright cloud covered them, and a voice from the cloud said, "This is my Son, whom I love; with him I am well pleased. Listen to him!"

*When the disciples heard this, they fell face
down to the ground, terrified. But Jesus came
and touched them. "Get up," he said. "Don't be
afraid." When they looked up, they saw no one
except Jesus.* (Matthew 17:1-8)

Take time to read these verses through a couple of
times, preferably aloud. First time round, read it at your
normal pace. Second time round, read it slowly, savouring each phrase.

- *As we did with Luke's version, see if you can spot
  what's distinctive about Matthew's account.*

MONDAY

His face shone like the sun.

MATTHEW 17:2

66 I t's your time to shine," we sometimes say. Perhaps a child is about to perform in a show. Perhaps it's a friend's first day at work. We all want to shine—to do well, to be radiant, to light up the room.

The transfiguration was Jesus' time to shine. As we've seen, it was a picture of his final victory. One day, he will light up the whole world. But what about us? Do we have a time to shine?

Jesus once told the story of a farmer who sowed wheat in his field. Nothing unusual about that. But an enemy came and scattered weed seeds in the field. So, when the plants first began to sprout, a profusion of weeds was growing amongst the wheat. The farmer's workforce suggested pulling up the weeds. But the man himself didn't want to risk good plants being pulled up along with the bad. So everything was left until harvest time. Then the weeds would be collected and burnt, and the wheat brought safely into the barn (Matthew 13:24-30).

The disciples weren't quite sure what to make of this story. So Jesus explained it to them (v 36-43). The farmer is Jesus himself, the field is his world and the good seed represents his people. Meanwhile the enemy is the devil and the weeds are those who side with the devil against God. The harvest is the final judgment at the end of the age.

So the meaning of the parable is that at the moment the kingdoms of Jesus and Satan co-exist in this world. Jesus has delayed the defeat of Satan's kingdom so that people have an opportunity to repent before it's too late. But a final judgment is coming. "The Son of Man will send out his angels," comments Jesus, "and they will weed out of his kingdom everything that causes sin and all who do evil" (v 41). The burning of the weeds is a picture of the fate of all those who reject Jesus.

But what about those who put their faith in Jesus? What will their fate be? Jesus says, "Then the righteous will *shine like the sun* in the kingdom of their Father" (v 43).

Only Matthew includes this parable. Then a little later, when he describes the transfiguration, only Matthew tells us that the face of Jesus "shone like the sun" (17:2). Matthew clearly wants to link the story of the transfiguration with the parable of the weeds. The point is this: one day the faces of believers will shine like the sun just as the transfigured face of Jesus shone like the sun. We see something of our future in the transfiguration of Jesus. The face of Jesus shining like the sun is a promise of the faces of Christians shining like the sun at the end of the age. *We will be transfigured.*

The medieval theologian Anselm says that at the transfiguration Jesus "gave a pre-view of his own glory and of the glory of his own".[36] Jesus is prefiguring *our* transfiguring.

MEDITATION

*The foundation was laid [in the transfiguration]
of the Holy Church's hope,
that the whole body of Christ might realize
the character of the change which it would have to receive,
and that the members might promise themselves
a share in that honour which had already
shone forth in their Head.*

(The 5th-century theologian and pope Leo the Great)[37]

TUESDAY

*Then you will shine among them
like stars in the sky.*

PHILIPPIANS 2:15

The story of the transfiguration is about to take an astonishing twist: it's your turn to be transfigured. The word traditionally translated "transfigured" in the Gospels is the same word translated elsewhere as "transformed":

Romans 12:2:

"Do not conform to the pattern of this world, but be *transformed* by the renewing of your mind."

2 Corinthians 3:18:

"And we all, who with unveiled faces contemplate the Lord's glory, are being *transformed* into his image with ever-increasing glory, which comes from the Lord, who is the Spirit."

We *will be* transformed or transfigured in the future. We *will* reflect the glory of Jesus. "We know that when Christ appears, we shall be like him, for we shall see him as he is" (1 John 3:2).

But Romans 12 and 2 Corinthians 3 both describe a process that has *already begun*. Romans 12:2 is a call to stop mirroring the sinful culture around us, and instead to be transformed—or transfigured—by the renewing of our minds. Paul isn't telling the church in Rome about a future transformation; he's calling them to action in the present. And 2 Corinthians 3:18, too, describes a transformation that is happening here and now: we "*are being* transformed". We're being transfigured "from one degree of glory to another" (ESV). When Christ returns, that transformation will be complete—our glory will be on another level. But already we're being transfigured as we contemplate the glory of Christ.

You are being transfigured! Pause and think about that for a moment.

The face of Jesus *literally* shone like the sun on the mount of transfiguration. Perhaps our faces will radiate light—or perhaps reflect the light of Christ—when Christ returns. But for now our transfiguration is moral rather than physical.

The apostle Paul writes, "Do all things without grumbling or disputing, that you may be blameless and innocent, children of God without blemish in the midst of a crooked and twisted generation, among whom *you shine as lights in the world*, holding fast to the word of life" (Philippians 2:14-16, ESV). Here again is a promise that we will shine as we hold fast to God's word. What does that look like? It looks like not grumbling or disputing. Perhaps that feels a bit down-to-earth after the radiant glory of the transfiguration. But actually, it's no less extraordinary and no less miraculous. We live "in the midst of a crooked and twisted generation". Grumbling and disputing are most people's default setting. To turn that around takes nothing less than a mighty work of the Almighty God. It might not seem like much, but in the darkness of our sinful culture, it means we shine like stars.

The 6th-century abbot Anastasius of Sinai asks, "What is greater or more awe-inspiring than this: to see God in human form, his face shining like the sun and even more brightly than the sun, flashing with light, ceaselessly sending forth rays, radiating splendour?" The answer is surely: "Nothing!" Nothing is more amazing than God-made-flesh shining like the sun.

But no, says Anastasius. It turns out there is something even more amazing. The most amazing thing is this:

> *To see [Jesus] raising his immaculate finger in the direction of his own face, pointing with it, and saying to those with him there: "So shall the just shine in the resurrection; so shall they be glorified, changed to reveal this form of mine, transfigured to this level of glory, stamped with this form, made like to this image, to this impress, to this light, to this blessedness, and becoming enthroned with me, the Son of God."*[38]

MEDITATION

Focus and raise the eye of your mind, I beg you,
towards the light of the gospel message,
so that you may be "transformed" in this time
"by the renewal of your minds".
In this way, clinging to that brilliant vision above,
you will become conformed to the
likeness of the glory of the Lord,
whose face shone on the mountain today like the sun.

(The 14th-century theologian Gregory of Palamas)

WEDNESDAY

With unveiled faces...

2 CORINTHIANS 3:18

Come back with me to when I was a young boy in "the olden days". As we travel back in time, we leave behind the age of smart watches that connect to your phone. We come to the age of digital watches with a faint back-light illuminating the watch face. But then we have to leave even this era of human civilisation. We come to a day when the height of technological sophistication was the luminous watch—one of my prized possessions as a boy. The hands of my luminous watch—and, yes, it had an analogue face—were coated in a mysterious substance that glowed in the dark. It was probably radioactive, but health and safety standards were not what they are today! Photons in natural light were stored in the photoluminescent coating and then emitted again in the dark. It absorbed light and then emitted light.

It's a process that reminds me of what happened to Moses on Mount Sinai, and today we come back to his story. Exodus 34:29-30 says:

When Moses came down from Mount Sinai, with
the two tablets of the testimony in his hand as he
came down from the mountain, Moses did not
know that the skin of his face shone because he had
been talking with God. Aaron and all the people
of Israel saw Moses, and behold, the skin of his
face shone, and they were afraid to come near him.
(Exodus 34:29-30, ESV)

As we've seen, Matthew uses the same language to describe Jesus at the transfiguration: "His face shone" (Matthew 17:2). And he uses the same language to describe God's people: "The righteous will shine like the sun" (13:43). The big difference between Jesus and us is that the radiant glory of Jesus is *inherent*. On Mount Sinai, Moses encountered God's glory, and in some way that glory became imprinted into his skin—like light on the hands of a luminous watch. But on the mount of transfiguration, Jesus himself was the source of glory.

Nevertheless, the promise implicit in the transfiguration is that Jesus will share his glory with us. As we see the glory of God in Christ, so we will become radiant with that glory. We reflect out the glory we have received from Jesus. Our faces will shine and our lives will shine.

This idea is picked up by Paul in 2 Corinthians 3 where Paul recounts the story of Moses on Mount Sinai. He concludes, "And we all, who with unveiled faces contemplate the Lord's glory, are being transformed [transfigured] into his image with ever-increasing glory" (2 Corinthians 3:18). Like Moses and like Jesus, we too can be transfigured. How? By contemplating the glory of Christ displayed in the light of the gospel (4:4).

As we gaze upon Christ, we are transfigured by our encounter with his glory. His glory captures our hearts and reorders our affections. We become entranced by the beauty of the one we see in the pages of Scripture. We become radiant people who shine with the glory of the grace of Christ.

MEDITATION

I heard the voice of Jesus say,
"I am this dark world's Light;
Look unto me, your morn shall rise,
And all your day be bright!"
I looked to Jesus, and I found
In him my Star, my Sun;
And in that Light of life I'll walk,
Till trav'ling days are done.

(From "I heard the voice of Jesus say" by Horatius Bonar)

THURSDAY

So shall we bear the image of the heavenly man.

1 CORINTHIANS 15:49

As a child I used to collect frog spawn. I loved watching the eggs turn into tadpoles, and watching the tadpoles turn into little frogs. On one occasion I found a chrysalis which I then put on my bedroom windowsill. Of course, one day I woke to find I was sharing my room with a butterfly. The Greek word for "transfiguration" is *metamorphosis*, a word that has entered the English language to describe the complete transformation of an animal—from a tadpole into a frog or from a chrysalis into a butterfly.

Becoming a Christian initiates a process which ends with our transformation into something as beautiful as a butterfly. It's not that we change from being human to something else. The butterfly is not a different animal from the caterpillar who created the chrysalis and the frog in your garden is the same creature as the tadpole from which it emerged. Our "metamorphosis" does not make us less human, nor transform us into some other kind of being. No, our broken humanity is restored so we become human as we were meant to be, perfectly imaging God. Hywel Jones says, "Transfiguration [of Jesus] shows how the divine can penetrate the human without destroying it. Transformation [of Christians] shows how the human can become conformed to the divine without its ceasing to be human."[39]

So, theologian Michael Allen says, "Sanctification involves transfiguration, not transubstantiation". Transubstantiation is the Roman Catholic belief that the Communion bread and wine cease to be bread and wine (though retaining the visible form of bread and wine). The claim is that the inner essence of the bread and wine are transformed into the physical body and blood of Jesus. The Protestant Reformers rejected this. The bread remains bread and the wine remains wine, but Christ is communicated to us by the Holy Spirit in the Lord's Supper with the bread and wine acting as physical signs or tokens of Christ's presence and promise.[40]

Transubstantiation does not describe what happens in Communion. But neither, argues Allen, does it describe what happens as God changes us (the process of "sanctification"). "As with transfiguration, the substance of the human remains definitively human … Unlike transubstantiation, the human form does not mask something miraculously other and divergent or heterogeneous in its character". In other words, we don't stop being human. It's not that some part of our humanity is substituted and replaced by a bit of divinity. Instead, "as with transfiguration, the human bears witness to the presence of something greater than itself, the very indwelling of

God's own Holy Spirit conforming the human unto the creaturely image of God's own Son".[41] The presence of the Holy Spirit does not replace our humanity. Quite the opposite. It makes us truly human, human as we were always meant to be.

So the possibility of growth and change in this present life is promised in the transfiguration.

We can go further. Hywel Jones says the transfiguration is also the promise of our glorification in the next life. "It is Jesus the man who is transfigured," he says, "and that demonstrates that human nature is capable of bearing the divine glory".[42] Paul himself says, "Just as we have borne the image of the earthly man, so shall we bear the image of the heavenly man" (1 Corinthians 15:49). So Jones concludes, "Jesus transfigured is the guarantee of every Christian's transformation".[43] This is what we have to look forward to. When our human bodies are faltering and failing, we can draw strength from this promise from God.

MEDITATION

"The Transfiguration is a glimpse
of Man's proper destiny."

(Michael Ramsey)[44]

GOOD FRIDAY

God demonstrates his own love for us in this:
while we were still sinners, Christ died for us.

ROMANS 5:8

On Good Friday we remember the death of Jesus. Often when we commemorate a person's death we actually focus on their life—we remember what they did rather than how they died. But on Good Friday the focus is very much on the death of Jesus—its how and why. For Jesus didn't die peacefully in his sleep or at the end of a struggle against cancer or even heroically in battle. He died a deliberate, violent, cruel, humiliating death. As far as the Roman authorities were concerned, he was executed as a criminal. As far as the Jewish authorities were concerned, he was cursed by God as a blasphemer.

What, then, is the true meaning of his death?

First, the cross reveals human sin. Jesus had lived a life of love: healing the sick, providing for the poor, standing up for justice. But humanity rejected him. When we had the opportunity, we murdered our Creator. Our attitude to God is displayed on the cross of Calvary. Our inner rebellion is projected onto the screen of history for all to see.

But second, the cross reveals God's love. Human beings killed Jesus, but they did so as part of a divine plan (Acts 4:27-28). Jesus didn't have his life wrenched from him; he laid it down of his own accord (John 10:18). The only way God could welcome guilty sinners was through the cross. Because God is just, he must punish our crimes—the penalty must be paid. Because God is love, Jesus was punished in our place—the penalty was paid on our behalf. In love the Father gave his Son, and in love the Son gave himself, through the enabling power of the Spirit. God's love was projected onto the screen of history for all to see (Romans 5:8).

This is what makes Good Friday "good". Good Friday is the culmination of an eternal plan, conceived in love, activated at the incarnation, and completed through the cross and resurrection. It's a plan to rescue people from their sin and brokenness. Through the cross we can be forgiven, justified and reconciled with God. And therefore we can have hope. Without the cross, our future is the darkness of judgment. But if we embrace the message of the cross with its offer of forgiveness, then our future is the light of glory.

This is where the transfiguration comes in. It reminds us of what Good Friday was for: it was for glory. The cross is the crowning glory of Jesus. Heaven itself sings that Jesus is worthy. Why? They sing, "Because you were slain, and with your blood you purchased for God persons from every tribe and language and people and nation" (Revelation 5:9). The glory of Jesus on the mount of transfiguration is a picture of the glory of Jesus for ever.

But the transfiguration is also the promise of *our* glory if we entrust ourselves to Jesus. The future of Jesus glimpsed in the transfiguration has become the future of his people. On the night before he died, just before he went to the Garden of Gethsemane—where we are told he was greatly distressed (Mark 14:33-34)—Jesus prayed for all who would believe in him, people like you if you're a Christian. He said, "I have given them the glory that you gave me" (John 17:22). We experience a measure of glory now in the gospel. But Jesus went on, "Father, I want those you have given me to be with me where I am, and to see my glory" (John 17:24). The new creation will be glorious—a world without death or suffering or tears. But it will not be the golden pavements or crystal seas that captivate us. In all creation, what will hold our attention more than anything else will be the person of Jesus. And in Jesus, perhaps what will hold our attention most will be the wounds of love still visible in his hands and feet. We are moving from glory to glory, from glory reflected as in a mirror to glory face-to-face (1 Corinthians 13:12).

MEDITATION

For Jesus, the trauma is past:
he has entered into his rest.
For us, it is not past.
We are still struggling and suffering.
To that situation the transfiguration still speaks,
because it discloses not only the glory
eternally possessed by the Lord,
and not only the glory for which, as
incarnate Mediator, he was destined,
but also the glory of his people ...
The transfiguration showed not only
what he would become
but what we would become.

(Donald Macleod)[45]

HOLY SATURDAY

For you were once darkness, but now you are light in the Lord. Live as children of light.

EPHESIANS 5:8

"Holy Saturday"—the day between Good Friday and Easter Sunday—is a day of darkness. In the Eastern Orthodox tradition, the day ends with all the lights being extinguished. We are left waiting for the light of Easter morning to break through.

Of course, as Christians, we know how the story ends. We follow the final days of the life and death of Jesus knowing that Easter is coming. We know the ultimate happy-ever-after is on its way.

But Holy Saturday reminds us that we're not there yet. Yes, Christ has risen. But physical resurrection is not yet our experience, nor the experience of creation. Christ is the firstfruits, but the harvest is still to come. In this present age, we live, as it were, between Good Friday and Easter Sunday; between death and eternal life; in the old age of this world, yet waiting for the dawn of the coming age. We're nearly there. It's as if the resurrection of Jesus is the first chink of light on the horizon, the sign that a new day is coming. Soon. But not yet.

In Romans 13:12 Paul says, "The night is nearly over; the day is almost here. So let us put aside the deeds of darkness and put on the armour of light." We still live in the night-time of this broken world. But the daytime of God's new world is almost here. This is our hope and comfort in dark times.

But Paul's main point is that as Christians we're to live as citizens of the *coming* age, not as citizens of this present passing age. Darkness is often associated with nefarious activities. It's a time for crime, conspiracies and illicit liaisons. So it's an apt picture of the sinful way of life we're to leave behind as we head towards the coming age. We belong to light and so we're to live as children of light (Ephesians 5:8).

The 14th-century theologian Gregory of Palamas links the transfiguration to Romans 13:12:

> "Let us then put away the works of darkness," brothers and sisters, "and let us do the works of light" (Rom. 13:12) so that we may not only walk nobly, as in this present day, but may also become "children of the day" (1 Thess. 5:5). Come, then, let us climb the mountain where Christ shone forth, so that we may see what is there; or rather, the Word of God himself will, in due time, lead us up [the mountain], since we have become people of this kind, worthy of such a day.[46]

The transfiguration is an invitation to see the light of the coming day radiating from the face of Jesus. And then to live as people of the light. So ask him to help you shine brightly today.

MEDITATION

Jesus said:
"You are the light of the world.
A town built on a hill cannot be hidden.
Neither do people light a lamp and put it
under a bowl.
Instead they put it on its stand,
and it gives light to everyone in the house.
In the same way, let your light shine before others,
that they may see your good deeds
and glorify your Father in heaven."

(Matthew 5:14-16)

EASTER SUNDAY

"Get up," he said. "Don't be afraid."

MATTHEW 17:7

The transfiguration, says Michael Ramsey, "stands as a gateway to the saving events of the Gospel, and is as a mirror in which the Christian mystery is seen in its unity".

He acknowledges the fact that the transfiguration does not belong to the central core of the gospel. There are no examples in the book of Acts of the transfiguration being part of the apostolic preaching. And yet, writes Ramsey, the transfiguration brings together so many truths that are central to our faith. As Ramsey gives examples, he summarises much that we have seen as we've looked at the transfiguration from different angles:

> *Here we perceive that the living and the dead are one in Christ, that the old covenant and the new are inseparable, that the Cross and the glory are of one, that the age to come is already here, that our human nature has a destiny of glory, that in Christ the final word is uttered and in Him*

alone the Father is well pleased. Here the diverse elements in the theology of the New Testament meet. Forgetfulness of the truths for which the Transfiguration stands has often led to distortions … Against these distortions the Transfiguration casts its light in protest.[47]

Where does this leave us?

In Mark's account of the story the disciples are afraid when Jesus is transfigured. In Luke's account the fear comes when the cloud covers them. But in Matthew's account, the disciples are afraid when "a voice speaks from the cloud". It's an echo of Deuteronomy 5:22-27 where Moses reminds the Israelites of what happened at Mount Sinai. The people heard a voice from the cloud and feared they would be consumed by divine fire (Exodus 20:19-20). Now the disciples hear a voice from a cloud and are filled with fear. When the transfiguration is depicted in traditional icons, the disciples lie prostrate on the ground, angled away from Jesus as if thrown to the floor by the "blast" of his radiance.

What happens next? Matthew says, "When the disciples heard this, they fell face down to the ground, terrified. But Jesus came and touched them. 'Get up,' he said. 'Don't be afraid'" (Matthew 17-6:7). It's the only time Jesus himself speaks in the story. "Get up." "Don't be afraid." Michael Ramsey says, "As at Sinai, it is the voice that makes them afraid … The scene quivers with an awe like the awe of Sinai. Only Jesus can free them from their fear, and He comes and bids them to fear not."[48]

The word translated "get up" (NIV) or "rise" (ESV) is related to the word for resurrection. The disciples "fell face down to the ground" like dead men and Jesus says, *Rise up*. It's almost as if the gospel story is enacted in this moment. Sinful human beings must fall before divine glory. That's what happened at the cross: Jesus fell, not only to the ground but into the grave. Then three days later he rose again. But he died and rose on our behalf. He was the firstborn from among the dead, the first of many. Those who are his rise with him.

And we rise to a life without fear. "Don't be afraid," says Jesus at the transfiguration (v 7). He says exactly the same thing after his resurrection. The first words of the risen Christ are: "Do not be afraid" (28:10). Do not be afraid because Jesus has risen. Death is defeated. Sin is forgiven. God and humanity are reconciled. The voice of God need no longer fill us with fear. Now the voice of God says to us, to you, *Get up, rise up, do not be afraid*.

- *Do not fear judgment, for the sacrifice for sin has been accepted.*

- *Do not fear death, for the grave is empty.*

- *Do not fear shame, for Jesus has risen to justify his people.*

- *Do not fear Satan, for Satan has been stripped of his power.*

- *Do not fear other people, for Jesus has risen as Lord over all.*

- *Do not fear loss for the resurrection is the promise of an eternal inheritance.*

- *Do not fear the future for the future is Jesus.*

MEDITATION

"The LORD bless you
and keep you;
the LORD make his face shine on you
and be gracious to you;
the LORD turn his face towards you
and give you peace."

(Numbers 6:24-26)

ENDNOTES

1 Adapted from "Discourse of our Holy Father Gregory the Sinaite on the Holy Transfiguration of our Lord Jesus Christ", in Brian E. Daley (ed. and trans.), *Light on the Mountain: Greek Patristic and Byzantine Homilies on the Transfiguration of the Lord* (St. Vladimir's Press, 2013), p 348-349, with allusions to Psalm 36:7-9.

2 John Calvin, *Calvin's Commentaries: A Harmony of the Gospels Matthew, Mark and Luke Volume II*, David W. Torrance and Thomas F. Torrance (eds.), T. H. L. Parker (trans.) (Saint Andrew Press, 1972), p 198-199.

3 Martin Luther, *Sermons on the Gospel of St John: Chapters 14-16, Luther's Works, 24:65-66*; cited in John W. Kleinig, *Wonderfully Made: A Protestant Theology of the Body* (Lexham Press, 2021), p 81-82.

4 See Stephen Williams, "The Transfiguration of Jesus Christ Part 2: Approaching Sonship", *Themelios 28.2* (Spring 2003), p 20.

5 D.A. Carson, "Matthew" in *Matthew, Mark Luke*, The Expositor's Bible Commentary Volume 8, Frank E. Gaebelein (ed.) (Zondervan, 1984), p 385.

6 A. Michael Ramsey, *The Glory of God and the Transfiguration of Christ* (Longmans, 1949), p 120.

7 Leontius, "Homily on the Transfiguration of Our Lord Jesus Christ", in Brian E. Daley (ed. and trans.), *Light on the Mountain* (as above), p 126.

8 James R. Edwards, *The Gospel According to Mark*, Pillar New Testament Commentary (Apollos, 2002), p 266.

9 Martin Luther, Sermons on the Gospel of St John (as above); cited in John W. Kleinig, *Wonderfully Made* (as above), p 81-82.

10 Anastasius of Sinai, "Homily on the Transfiguration", in Brian E. Daley (ed. and trans.), *Light on the Mountain* (as above), p 172.

11 John Calvin, *Calvin's Commentaries: A Harmony of the Gospels Matthew, Mark and Luke Volume II* (as above), p 198, 200.

12 Joel B. Green, *The Gospel of Luke,* New International Commentary on the New Testament (Eerdmans, 1997), p 380.

13 A. Michael Ramsey, *The Glory of God and the Transfiguration of Christ* (as above), p 119.

14 Cited in A. Michael Ramsey (as above), p 137.

15 Kathryn Tanner; cited in Michael Allen, *Sanctification,* New Studies in Dogmatics (Zondervan, 2017), p 216.

16 Anastasius of Sinai, "Homily on the Transfiguration," in Brian E. Daley (ed. and trans.), *Light on the Mountain* (as above), p 165, citing Genesis 3:21 and Psalm 104:2.

17 John Calvin, *Calvin's Commentaries: A Harmony of the Gospels Matthew, Mark and Luke Volume II* (as above), p 199.

18 Leo the Great, "Sermon 51: A Homily Delivered on the Saturday Before the Second Sunday in Lent on the Transfiguration, Matthew 17:1-13", in *The Nicene and Post-Nicene Fathers: Second Series, Volume 12*, Philip Schaff and Henry Wace (eds.) (Hendrickson, 1994), p 163.

19 Leontius, "Homily on the Transfiguration of Our Lord Jesus Christ," in Brian E. Daley (ed. and trans.), *Light on the Mountain* (as above), p 120-121.

20 Pantoleon, "Sermon on the Most Glorious Transfiguration of Our Lord and God, Jesus Christ", in Brian E. Daley (as above), p 111.

21 Timothy of Antioch, "Homily of the Cross and the Transfiguration of Our Lord Jesus Christ", in Brian E. Daley (as above), p 151.

22 Timothy of Antioch, "Homily of the Cross and the Transfiguration of Our Lord Jesus Christ", in Brian E. Daley (as above), p 148.

23 Leo the Great, "Sermon 51: A Homily Delivered on the Saturday Before the Second Sunday in Lent on the Transfiguration, Matthew 17:1-13," in *The Nicene and Post-Nicene Fathers: Second Series, Volume 12* (as above), p 163.

24 Thomas Manton, *Works of Thomas Manton Volume 1* (Banner of Truth, 1993), p 356.

25 Philagathos, "Homily 31: On the Saving Transfiguration", in Brian E. Daley (ed. and trans.), *Light on the Mountain* (as above), p 263.

26 Rowan Williams, *The Dwelling of the Light* (Canterbury Press, 2003), p 10-11.

27 Robert Murray McCheyne, "The Transfiguration of Christ", *A Basket of Fragments: Notes for Revival* (Christian Focus, 2019), p 103-104.

28 "Discourse of our Holy Father Gregory the Sinaite on the Holy Transfiguration of our Lord Jesus Christ," in Brian E. Daley (ed. and trans.), *Light on the Mountain* (as above), p 327.

29 Joseph Hall, *Contemplations on the Historical Passages of the Old and New Testaments* (Nelson and Sons, 1868), p 517.

30 Thomas Aquinas, *Catena Aurea: Commentary of the Four Gospels*; cited in Hans Boersma, *Seeing God: The Beatific Vision in Christian Tradition* (Eerdmans, 2018), p 137.

31 Peter G. Bolt, *The Cross from a Distance: Atonement in Mark's Gospel*, New Studies in Biblical Theology No. 18 (Apollos, 2004), p 166.

32 Donald Macleod, *The Person of Christ* (IVP, 1998), p 105.

33 D.A. Carson, "*Matthew*" in *Matthew, Mark, Luke*, The Expositor's Bible Commentary Volume 8, Frank E. Gaebelein (ed.) (as above), p 384.

34 Basil, "Homily on Psalm 45:5"; cited in A. Michael Ramsey, *The Glory of God and the Transfiguration of Christ* (as above), p 131.

35 Jonathan Edwards, "Pure in Heart Blessed", *Works of Jonathan Edwards Online, Volume 17, Sermons and Discourses 1730-1733*, Mark Valeri (ed.) (Yale, 1999), p 66.

36 Anselm, cited in A. Michael Ramsey, *The Glory of God and the Transfiguration of Christ* (as above), p 132; and translated in Donald Macleod, *The Person of Christ* (IVP, 1998), p 107.

37 Leo the Great, "Sermon 51: A Homily Delivered on the Saturday Before the Second Sunday in Lent on the Transfiguration, Matthew 17:1-13," in *The Nicene and Post-Nicene Fathers: Second Series, Volume 12* (as above), p 163.

38 Anastasius of Sinai, "Homily on the Transfiguration," in Brian E. Daley (ed. and trans.), *Light on the Mountain* (as above), p 176.

39 Hywel R. Jones, *Transfiguration and Transformation* (Banner of Truth, 2021), p xvi.

40 See Tim Chester, *Truth We Can Touch: How Baptism and Communion Shape Our Lives* (Crossway, 2020).

41 Michael Allen, *Sanctification* (as above), p 225.

42 Hywel R. Jones, *Transfiguration and Transformation* (as above), p 56.

43 Hywel R. Jones (as above), p 56.

44 A. Michael Ramsey, *The Glory of God and the Transfiguration of Christ* (as above), p 142.

45 Donald Macleod, *The Person of Christ* (IVP, 1998), p 107.

46 Gregory of Palamas, "Homily 35: For the Same Transfiguration of the Lord", Section 4, in Brian E. Daley (ed. and trans.), *Light on the Mountain* (as above), p 369.

47 A. Michael Ramsey, *The Glory of God and the Transfiguration of Christ* (as above), p 144.

48 A. Michael Ramsey (as above), p 120-121.

the good book

C O M P A N Y

BIBLICAL | RELEVANT | ACCESSIBLE

At The Good Book Company, we are dedicated to helping Christians and local churches grow. We believe that God's growth process always starts with hearing clearly what he has said to us through his timeless word—the Bible.

Ever since we opened our doors in 1991, we have been striving to produce Bible-based resources that bring glory to God. We have grown to become an international provider of user-friendly resources to the Christian community, with believers of all backgrounds and denominations using our books, Bible studies, devotionals, evangelistic resources, and DVD-based courses.

We want to equip ordinary Christians to live for Christ day by day, and churches to grow in their knowledge of God, their love for one another, and the effectiveness of their outreach.

Call us for a discussion of your needs or visit one of our local websites for more information on the resources and services we provide.

Your friends at The Good Book Company